D0757203

After the Election

After the Election

Prophetic Politics in a Post-Secular Age

RON SANDERS

Foreword by
Scotty McLennan

 CASCADE *Books* · Eugene, Oregon

AFTER THE ELECTION
Prophetic Politics in a Post-Secular Age

Cascade Books
An Imprint of Wipf and Stock Publishers
199 W. 8th Ave., Suite 3
Eugene, OR 97401

www.wipfandstock.com

PAPERBACK ISBN: 978-1-5326-0120-0
HARDCOVER ISBN: 978-1-5326-0122-4
EBOOK ISBN: 978-1-5326-0121-7

New Revised Standard Version Bible, copyright 1989, Division of Christian Education of the National Council of the Churches of Christ in the United States of America. Used by permission. All rights reserved.

Cataloguing-in-Publication data:

Names: Sanders, Ron, author. | McLennan, Scotty, foreword.

Title: After the election : prophetic politics in a post-secular age / Ron Sanders ; foreword by Scotty McLennan.

Description: Eugene, OR : Cascade Books, 2018 | Includes bibliographical references and index.

Identifiers: ISBN 978-1-5326-0120-0 (paperback) | ISBN 978-1-5326-0122-4 (hardcover) | ISBN 978-1-5326-0121-7 (ebook)

Subjects: LCSH: Christianity and politics—United States. | Christians—Political activity—United States.

Classification: BR516 .S26 2018 (print) | BR516 .S26 (ebook)

Manufactured in the U.S.A.   APRIL 4, 2018

For Bonnie, Zac, and Sarah

Contents

Foreword

Scotty McLennan

THIS IS AN IMPORTANT BOOK. That is true not only for evangelical Christians, the tradition with which Ron Sanders identifies, but also for the rest of us: liberal Christians like myself, people of other religious traditions, the "spiritual but not religious," those whose religious preference is "none," secularists, and atheists. My friend Ron knowledgeably, articulately, and compellingly describes a positive path forward for politics and religion in America. This seems an almost-impossible task in an era of electoral bitterness, culture wars, religiously inspired hatred and violence, and aggressive "New Atheism." My parents always told me that there were two things never to discuss publicly, at least in polite company: politics and religion. Ron has taken them on together and done a resplendent job of showing us how to converse about them, live them out, and build a flourishing society around them.

Ron convincingly describes how modern democracy and Christianity grew up together, complement each other, and need each other, now more than ever. The liberal democratic tradition, which is foundational to America, is the best way to organize our pluralistic society, giving voice to many different communities. Yet, it provides only a thin ethic of "Do no harm," setting up certain procedural safeguards for how citizens relate to each other but ultimately furthering the power of the majority to enforce its will. Christianity, on the other hand, risks becoming absolutist, uncompromising and oppressive if it dominates in the political realm—hence, the importance of church-state separation—but it can also positively supply a thick narrative and exemplary ethic of love where democracy simply referees competing values in society. If the two are actively allowed to

complement each other through a creative blurring of strict lines of separation between church and state, both flourish in a way they could not in the
absence of the other.

Ron and I have long discussed and debated these issues, publicly and
privately, in our years at Stanford University, beginning for me in 2001. We
have spent a lot of time talking together in cafes, reading and comment-
ing on each other's papers and book drafts, helping guide students through
difficult dormitory discussions about religion, standing side by side at
public demonstrations, serving on interfaith councils together, and teaching together in the classroom. On many religious and political matters we
are one hundred and eighty degrees apart. He is a PhD graduate of Fuller
Theological Seminary and a staff member with Cru. I have degrees in law
and theology from Harvard and am a Unitarian Universalist minister (for-
merly a university chaplain at Stanford, and before that at Tufts, overseeing
all campus religious groups and ministries). He identifies as an evangelical
Christian, and I as a liberal mainline Christian. My politics are well to the
left of his in many areas. But we are good friends, colleagues, and discussion partners. I have learned a great deal from him in a decade and a half.

For example, in a public response to my 2009 book *Jesus Was a Liberal: Reclaiming Christianity for All* at the Stanford Memorial Church, he
challenged my four criteria for claiming that Jesus was a liberal: freedom
from religious authority, rationality as a primary way of knowing, belief in
the essential goodness of humanity, and tolerance for other ways than one's
own. He noted how Jesus established himself as authority, how rationality
is influenced by one's own preconceived notions and loyalties, how much
evil humans are capable of, and how traditional Christianity sees itself as
the only way to salvation.

Ron then went on to make claims that he expands upon masterfully in
this book. Jesus was probably a first-century liberal, in that he stood in the
great prophetic tradition of Israel, challenging the accepted conventions of
the day. He liberalized the traditional definition of who might be invited
into the kingdom of God. He might have had a prophetic word to say to
modern conservatives about setting up theological litmus tests to define
people in or out of the community, about taking the log out of one's own
eye before attending to the speck in another's eye, about being too authoritative when we all wander in the same desert. But Jesus might also have
had prophetic words for modern liberals about the importance of tradition,
about idolizing the individual and personal conscience, and about defining

people out of the intellectual community because they take the scriptures as a primary source of knowledge about what means the most to all of us. He concluded that Jesus prophetically challenges all of us at every theological and political turn, including Ron's own assumptions about Jesus and what it means to be a faithful follower of him. That is the virtue of humility as personified in Ron.

Another reason this is an important book is that it accessibly canvases the thought of major modern philosophers and theologians in helping us understand the relationship of politics and religion—among them Richard Rorty, Alasdair MacIntyre, Jeffrey Stout, Stanley Hauerwas, and John Howard Yoder. Richard Rorty represents the secularist position of guaranteeing religious liberty in people's private lives but keeping religion out of the public square, where it causes division and conflict. For Rorty, there are no capital-T or universal truths, and religion is ultimately misleading. Alasdair MacIntyre agrees that there are no capital-T truths, but he asserts a modest universalism based at first on particular communities' own understandings (often religious), which then become larger and broader as they stand the test of time and reach across communities in the public square. Jeffrey Stout sees that religion can be a positive force for good in the public square (for example, the Christianity of Reverend Martin Luther King Jr.). Stanley Hauerwas, however, wants to keep a clear separation between church and state, because once religion enters the public square he sees it getting corrupted by cultural dynamics and political power; an uncompromised Christian community can ideally be an exemplar of what human flourishing looks like. For John Howard Yoder, the Christian community should strive to remain uncompromised and uncorrupted, but still should engage in the political realm, reflecting Christian values like pacifism.

Ron explains in detail both the desire to keep church and state strictly separated (Rorty and Hauerwas, for different reasons) and the urge to blur the boundaries between church and state for their mutual benefit (MacIntyre, Stout, and Yoder). He then describes two fundamentally different images from ancient Israel of the role of Christianity in America—the new promised land for a chosen people that becomes a Christian nation, or a covenanted people who are living in exile under another realm's power. Ron sees the first image as a misguided mythology for America and the second as a genuinely Christian perspective. The political problem with the first is that it demolishes church-state separation in the name of Christian hegemony for the nation. The second maintains the possibilities both of church-state separation and of somewhat blurred boundaries.

There are good reasons to blur the boundaries for both the liberal democratic tradition and for Christianity, as Ron sees it. Democracy can be strengthened by faith-based voluntary associations that bring the marginalized into focus and provide creative and exemplary ways to minister to them; by moral response to unjust majoritarian state action, as with the Southern Christian Leadership Conference during the civil rights movement; and by development of Christian virtues like love, taking us beyond the core democratic value of preventing harm. On the other hand, Christianity can be strengthened if religious language and motives are introduced to the public conversation, where they can be challenged or nuanced; if religious traditions can be asked publicly to see their all-too-human dimensions of finiteness and self-service; and if they are pushed to hear voices that have been excluded from the Christian worldview so that empathy can be developed.

I would like to expand on Ron's arguments for blurring the church-state boundaries in the service of each. I believe that, historically, this has been done fairly well by an American notion of "civil religion," which Ron explains has been disparaged both by Richard Rorty's concern about retaining the purity of the liberal democratic tradition based solely on secular discourse and by Stanley Hauerwas's concern about washing out the particularities of being a follower of Jesus in the service of a generalized religious ethic promoted by the state.

It seems to me that the Declaration of Independence is the centerpiece of a civil religion in America. It reads, "We hold these truths to be self-evident, that all men are created equal, that they are endowed by their Creator with certain unalienable Rights, that among these are Life, Liberty and the pursuit of Happiness."[1] Stanford graduate and Unitarian Universalist minister Forrest Church has called this, in a book by the same name, "the American Creed." It states commitments to values of equality, liberty, and rights-based justice—not merely as a matter of principles of good government, but as having a transcendent source in the Laws of Nature and of Nature's God.

Clearly, as Ron points out in this book, we have historically fallen far short of fulfilling the values of the Declaration. African-American slaves were not considered men at the time slaveholder Thomas Jefferson penned

1. "Declaration of Independence," para. 2.

the document, and it took a long, bloody Civil War to settle that issue. Women were not included in the term "men," and women's equality, in terms of suffrage alone, took another 144 years. Much of this country was stolen outright from its indigenous inhabitants, who were herded as supposedly sovereign nations onto reservations. Martin Luther King Jr. had to invoke the Declaration of Independence again almost two hundred years later at the Lincoln Memorial, along with explicit biblical references, to talk about a dream of freedom not yet achieved.

Yet, it turns out that our creedal commitment to liberty as an inalienable right, as interpreted through the constitutional Bill of Rights, keeps atheist and agnostic liberty from being coerced by believers, just as much as it protects believers' rights to free exercise of their religion. Our American creed also protects liberty from itself, from it becoming such thoroughgoing individualism that we forget the transcendent referent that calls us together in covenanting community. It helps us to see ourselves as one nation, not just many individuals living in the same place—*e pluribus unum*—"out of many, one."

It also helps us in the face of religious fundamentalisms that challenge the alleged amorality of certain forms of modern secularism. Our civil religion can face down sectarian fundamentalist attempts to impose a different creed upon the body politic, and can also co-exist with many different forms of sectarian religion, which can be freely exercised as long as they don't try to become the established religion of the state.

Moreover, our American creed has given rise to a robust and respected tradition of civil disobedience, from Henry David Thoreau's refusal to pay war taxes to Martin Luther King's rejection of Jim Crow laws. Calvin Coolidge once said, you may "speak of natural rights, but I challenge anyone to show where in nature any rights existed." As Coolidge saw it, that is what positive laws established by legislatures are all about. Laws create rights, and they do not exist otherwise. That would mean that rights could just as easily be eliminated by legislators. Of course the Holocaust perpetrated by Nazi Germany was in large part based on duly passed laws, carefully administered by legally authorized agents of the state. Coolidge was wrong. The genius of American civil religion is that it produces moral checks and balances to positive law, whether created by legislators or by judges in the common-law tradition. It's on the basis of inalienable rights with which we're endowed by Nature's God that Martin Luther King could write from the Birmingham City Jail that "there are two types of laws: there are *just* and there are *unjust* laws . . . A just law is a man-made code that squares with the moral law or the law of God . . . An unjust law is a human law that is not rooted in eternal and natural law."[2] President Kennedy, in his Inaugural Address, after noting that "the same revolutionary beliefs for which our forebears fought are still at issue around the globe—the belief that the rights of man come not from the generosity of the state but from the hand of God," went on to say that "the trumpet summons us again . . . [to] struggle against the common enemies of man: tyranny, poverty, disease and war itself."[3]

Is it not our civil religion that holds us together, given our enormous diversity and our commitment to pluralism? We are constantly absorbing new immigrant populations. Many other countries are held together by an ethnic identity of being, say, Japanese, Turk, Chinese, Russian, Serbian, or French. Although America has arguably historically been a melting pot into a white, Anglo-Saxon, Protestant reality, that hasn't been our conscious self-image. Instead, we've pledged ourselves to "liberty and justice for all," and we have sung of "crowning thy good with brotherhood from sea to shining sea." That spirit of hospitality is picked up in the inscription on the base of the Statue of Liberty. Written by a Sephardic Jew, it reads, "Give me your tired, your poor, / Your huddled masses, yearning to breathe free, / The wretched refuse of your teeming shore. / Send these, the homeless, tempest-tost to me, / I lift my lamp beside the golden door!"

America is not an ethnicity, or even a people with a common history. As Jacob Needleman exclaims in his book *The American Soul*, "American [is] an *idea*! What other country can say that?"[4] Of course, our American civil religion is far from being fully realized. To say "God bless America," as presidents and presidential candidates inevitably seem to do in ending their speeches, should be a trembling statement of supplication, not an assumption of fact. It is not "America has God's blessing and we deserve it," but instead "*May* you, God, please bless America, by showing us your ways" and "*May* you shed your grace on us, sinners that we are, and help us to move closer to you." In Irving Berlin's 1938 song, "God Bless America," God is asked to stand beside America and to guide her.

I suggest that America should not be seen as a nation divided in the sense of conservatives and liberals, or religious people and secular people.

2. "King Papers," 7.

3. "John F. Kennedy Quotations," paras. 3, 23.

4. Needleman, "The American Soul," 46.

Our nation's soul is not divided, either. Instead, we have a civil religion that binds us together. Like any great myth or symbol, the idea of America has layers of meaning, and it's capable of holding opposites in creative tension. We are united by a few basic values inherent in the idea of America—like liberty, equality, hope for the future, and faith that Nature and Nature's God have endowed us with certain inalienable rights as human beings. Of course, we differ deeply over a number of political issues like abortion, marriage for same-sex couples, our wars around the world, and levels of taxation. Yet, we can base our arguments in the public square on this set of deeper values that make up American civil religion. We can have the same reference points for our disagreements. Great symbols and myths work by incorporating dichotomy and paradox, by having the breadth to embrace past, present, and future, and by providing a hopeful vision of transformation out on the horizon.

But Ron is not talking about the historical role of civil religion in this book. He has taken on the much more difficult task of proving why the liberal democratic tradition and evangelical Christianity need each other, right now, in America. That is why what he is saying is so important for all of us to read and understand. For we are, as he well-demonstrates, in a new post-secular age, with modernism and postmodernism in the rearview mirror. We have had two recent presidents, Republican and Democrat, who maintained a White House office for faith-based partnerships in the face of criticisms from the American Civil Liberties Union (of which I am a card-carrying member) and Americans United for Separation of Church and State that the Establishment clause of the Constitution is being violated. Our new president, reportedly supported by 80 percent of white evangelical Christians, has not been publicly known for his religious commitments, although he is a lifelong Presbyterian Christian and was attracted early in his life to the Reverend Norman Vincent Peal, his "power of positive thinking," and the effect Donald Trump claimed it had on his business success. He has worked in recent years with megachurch pastor and television evangelist Paula White, who has called him a born-again Christian. She and other conservative ministers sat on his campaign's Evangelical Executive Advisory Board. The issue of the relationship of church and state remains before us, starting in the highest political office in the land.

As Ron observes, we live in a time when people increasingly identify as spiritual but not religious; when they are wary of religion in the public square because its presumed absolutism runs counter to peaceful coexistence in our pluralistic country; when religiously-inspired violence is on the rise. Yet, the majority of us still think that religion has an important role in addressing social issues like poverty, war, environmental destruction, bigotry, family disintegration, sexual violence, and respect for life itself. Love is the cornerstone of the Christian message, Ron explains, and justice is its social manifestation. Religion needs to remain involved in politics, both to promote positive social change of the sort encouraged by Reverend Martin Luther King Jr. and to put its reasoning into the public square where it can be examined, challenged, criticized, and reformed. The metaphor for Christians cannot be inheritors of the Promised Land in America. Instead it must be that of exiles in a strange land, where spiritual allegiance is to the Jesus of unconditional love, then acted out in political life. Christianity must operate by way of example, not by legislation.

In all of this, I agree with Ron. I think that demonstrates how effectively he is able to reach across religious and political difference (since I differ with him profoundly in many areas) to build a thesis that could guide us to a genuinely new and fruitful way to think about religion and politics in America, and then to act on it. Ron combines the best of a deep philosophical mind and a heart of Christian faithfulness. His analysis is unusually broad-based, linking sociology, political science, natural science, literature, and history to theology and philosophy. And it happens that he is also a wonderful human being—kind, caring, open, honest, trustworthy, collaborative, and well-liked by all who know him. I bet you will like his book too.

Preface

The major problem with the invitation [to the gospel] now is precisely overfamiliarity. Familiarity breeds unfamiliarity—unsuspected unfamiliarity, and then contempt. People think they have heard the invitation. They think they have accepted it—or rejected it. But they have not.

—Dallas Willard[5]

THE FIRST TIME I noticed that evangelical Christians were passionate about politics was 1988. I was a junior in college at Montana State University, traveling to Knoxville, Tennessee, to visit a friend. This was the first time that I was old enough to vote, but I forgot to file for an absentee ballot and had inadvertently scheduled my flight for election day. More importantly, I had recently had a deeply spiritual conversion experience to faith in Christ and was learning the ins and outs of what it meant to be an evangelical. On that day in 1988 one of the things that I learned was that evangelicals (and what I now know is "white evangelicals") vote Republican. When I landed and visited my friend in the dorms at the University of Tennessee, everyone was gathered around their televisions anticipating the results and rooting for George H. W. Bush to win the presidential election.

Over the course of time, I began to realize that political positions seemed to be a litmus test for Christian orthodoxy in America—at least evangelical Christian orthodoxy. I also learned that evangelicals cared deeply for America and its future. For many, this meant that the prosperity of America was tied to its faithfulness to legislate Christian morality: prayer in schools, the Ten Commandments in public places, being pro-life (except on the death penalty), etc. The fervor of these commitments was palpable

---

5. Willard, *Divine Conspiracy*, 11.

in many meetings and conferences that I attended. I was fairly new to this kind of faith and so I held this all loosely, but it was beginning to shape who I would listen to, the authors I would read, and the people I considered out of bounds when it came to matters of faith. At the same time, I had a Christian friend who was instrumental in my coming to faith who voted Democrat. What? This caused a little dissonance for me and was the first step in evaluating whether or not particular political platforms or parties had become attached to the good news of the gospel of Jesus.

I had such a deep and meaningful experience as a college student that I decided to come on staff with Cru so that I could talk to university students about what had happened in my life when I found faith in Christ. I have now been on staff for twenty-six years, and those years have mostly been great—such wonderful people who care deeply for others and have sacrificed much to help people grow in their spiritual lives. But over those twenty-six years I noticed an ever-increasing trend in my conversations with students and faculty. People had an interest in Jesus (and it was an almost overwhelmingly positive interest) but viewed Christianity as a religious tradition negatively. And while some people were attracted to Jesus, they could not imagine being a Christian, because the Christian faith that they saw on television, heard on the radio, or read about in newspapers and magazines was antithetical to their own politics. This has been especially true during the last seventeen years at Stanford University. When I was asked to speak on campus or participate in panels or forums concerning controversial social issues, it became clear that people expected at least three things from me as an evangelical. First, that I would tell them that they were wrong about something; evangelicals are largely perceived as against "most stuff." Second, that I would be judgmental towards them. And third, that I thought I had all the answers—to whatever questions anyone might have. So on one particularly contentious issue that I was asked to address I decided to do exactly the opposite of their expectations. I started with confession, what we as the church had done to marginalize and oppress certain groups of people in the past. Then I tried to emphasize how Christian morality should be voluntary and adopted from the ground up, and not legislated from the top down in a pluralistic society. Finally, I said that I did not know everything and could be wrong about some things—especially as it related to a biblical understanding of the particular issue and how it might be applied politically. After the event, there was an almost-unanimous response from the people that talked to me personally. They said, "You are an interesting Christian." I didn't know exactly what that meant, but after some reflection, I took it to mean that I did not quite fit their expectations of what an evangelical was supposed to say.

This experience and others would be the seed that would grow into my academic research in the PhD program in Christian Ethics at Fuller Theological Seminary. I wanted to test this hypothesis: the way evangelicals participated in politics over the last half-century has had a negative impact on how "outsiders" perceived the Christian faith. My advisors, Glen Stassen and Nancey Murphy, encouraged me in this direction, and this book is a result of my continued interest in this hypothesis. Five people stood out as I did my research. Michael Walzer, a Jewish political philosopher at Princeton's Institute for Advanced Studies, articulated an idea that still haunts me to this day (in a good way): that Christianity is at its best when it is creatively "setting the stage of history" (more on this later). Cornel West brought images of Christ's suffering on the cross into focus, and they expanded my understanding of the gospel. He also brought the richness of the Black Church tradition into his articulation of the democratic tradition in a way that I thought was interesting, and which challenged many of my assumptions about what authentic Christian faith looked like as a white evangelical. I had the opportunity to meet both men on separate occasions, and they were very generous to me in our short conversations. James Davison Hunter, a Christian Sociologist at the University of Virginia, put into words one of my frustrations—that the evangelical church's strategy for social change through politics seems misguided. And finally, both Dietrich Bonhoeffer and Martin Luther King Jr. were examples of prescient Christian faith in the face of injustice; they continue to be a source of inspiration in my field of Christian ethics.

There are more scholars than these: Richard Rorty, John Howard Yoder, Stanley Hauerwas, Jeffrey Stout, Nicholas Wolterstorff, and Alasdair MacIntyre all contributed to my understanding of the relationship between the democratic tradition and the Christian tradition. There is a risk in writing on people's views who are still working, and I hope that I got them right. Jeffrey Stout's generosity in reading my finished dissertation and his encouragement to use more of my own voice if I wanted to try to publish these ideas were very helpful.

There are also so many people to acknowledge and thank for their contribution to this project. The best of my work can be attributed to their influence—what is wrong or misguided is all from me. Glen and Nancey both challenged and guided me through my PhD, and their own faith journeys were encouraging and inspiring. My colleagues at Fuller Theological Seminary, past and present, helped me to become a better scholar. The faculty and staff at Fuller in the Bay Area were always supportive and encouraging as well. My good friend Reggie Williams was invaluable. His groundbreaking book *Bonhoeffer's Black Jesus* and this book were born out of our friendship and our many conversations about life, faith, Jesus, and Christian ethics. Scotty McLennan is a good friend and a colleague. He was the Dean of Religious Life at Stanford, and so I worked with him closely as I continued to minister on campus. His generosity as a person and to me as a minister at Stanford stood out as unique in my experience as an evangelical on campus. Our conversations at the faculty club always forced me to think more deeply about my own faith. As you read in the Foreword, we differ in some areas, but I think we would both say that we see Jesus differently because of our friendship. I want to thank him for taking time during his "retirement" to read the manuscript and contribute to this project.

My colleagues on Cru staff gave me feedback throughout this process and also gave me space in my work to write the manuscript. It is great when those above you are both generous and trusting. Thanks also to the folks at Wipf and Stock for taking a risk on a first-time author. This book is better because of their interest and work on the manuscript.

Several families helped me along the way: the Anthony family, the Burger family, the Knopf-Hansen family, the Park family, and the Younger family were all so encouraging, supportive, and would give me a place to write when I needed to focus. They are all the kinds of people that I have in mind when I think of how Christians should be living out their faith in the world. Three people helped to edit this project along the way. The ideas are mine, but the writing is better because of their influence: Brenna Peterson Rubio, Laura Ortberg Turner, and Kelsey Hanson Woodruff all contributed at some point. Kelsey helped in the final stages of completion as my research assistant and editor: she read the entire manuscript, gave me feedback, and worked to put it together before I sent it off to the publisher. She was an invaluable resource and has things to say of her own, so maybe someday I will be able to return the favor.

Finally, my extended family and my immediate family gave me the support and the love that was required to put some of these ideas "out there." They sacrificed quite a lot for me, and were a consistent reminder of why I started this project in the first place. My wife, Bonnie, and my kids,

Zac and Sarah, are all artists, and their creativity and compassion for people gives me hope for the future of Christian faith. They also would remind me on occasion that faith should be grounded in reality, so I should put down my books every once in a while, that failing is not failure unless you stop learning, and that a little whimsy makes for a more interesting life.

I haven't given up my evangelical faith or renounced the word "evangelical" to describe myself, despite all the baggage that comes along with it sometimes. On occasion, I will critique Evangelicalism, but it is an internal critique. We are not perfect as evangelicals, but these are my people. The substantive good that evangelicals are doing in the world sometimes gets overshadowed by some of our more sensational spokespersons. I hope that I captured a small shadow of that good. This book is meant to be a conversation starter. I think that Dallas Willard gets it right in the opening quotation—we think we are familiar with how Christianity and democracy should relate together, and that has resulted in an unfamiliarity, and sometimes in contempt. My argument is that this may be a time to revisit and renegotiate that relationship from both sides. There are two trajectories one can take with what I am trying to say in this book. First, is there room in the democratic tradition for a bit more blur between the church and the state, and what would that look like? I have offered a few proposals here, but as I argue, it is hardly a science. Second, what is the role of the Christian tradition in a pluralistic culture? I have focused most of my attention here because I think that if the Christian church can recover its distinctiveness as followers of Christ, it will discover under-realized resources for addressing some of our contemporary social problems.

Introduction

A Post-Secular Age

WE LIVE IN A post-secular age. Charles Taylor defines "secularity" in the West as a shift away from grounding reason and morality in a theistic worldview to theism being one of many possible alternatives for framing what it means to be human and live a good life.[1] Secularity, for Taylor, is charted along three planes: (1) the removal of the church from the state, (2) the ebbing tide of religious belief and practice in the West, and (3) the emerging background framework: the unspoken and taken-for-granted beliefs that shape what is possible to consider within a particular culture.[2]

One of the driving factors that contributed to this shift was the flurry of conflict that followed the Reformation. People grew weary of the absolutism and authoritarianism of state-sponsored religion in Western Europe that wedded the coercive power of the government with competing religious perspectives on theology and morality. The Reformed, Lutheran, and Catholic Christian traditions dominated the European landscape during the early stages of the Reformation period and vied for political and religious supremacy. Their competing moral and theological visions escalated into violence in the Thirty Years War and contributed to the Puritan revolution in England.[3] The difficulty maintaining social coherence in this milieu motivated the shift from an external order (one grounded in absolutism and theism) to a more internal order—based on human social cooperation. The coercive power of the state was wrested from the church (at least in

1. Taylor, *Secular Age*, 25.
2. Ibid., 13.
3. Hughes, *Myths America Lives By*, 47.

theory) and the just distribution of the goods of society placed in the hands of the people. This new way of picturing and practicing social existence—democracy—captured the imaginations of some of the great thinkers of the day.[4]

Christianity held a strong influence on the nascent stages of democracy as it developed in the West. Michael Walzer argues that Christianity, especially some of the tenets of Calvinist political philosophy in Western Europe, was a salve to the anxiety created as cultural tides shifted away from feudalism toward a more egalitarian approach to finding one's place in the world—especially in those nation-states dominated by Protestantism. Several key doctrines anchored the Christian impulses toward democracy. The doctrine of sin and total depravity helped shaped the notion of a balance of powers; no one person or group should hold exclusive power over citizens because of the potential to abuse that power. The Protestant doctrine of the "priesthood of all believers" challenged the feudal system and its inherited Greek ideology that everyone had a particular place in society. This leveled the playing field for more inclusion and participation in the political processes of government (although participation was still limited to male citizens, it did seed the impulse that would eventually lead to the participation of women and minority communities in the political process). The idea that church participation was chosen and not inherited also contributed to the notion of voluntary associations—people would gather for small-group Bible studies to encourage one another's growth in Christ. Christian commitments were to the church first when familial structures and obligations conflicted with loyalty to Christ. This would create an intellectual framework for smaller groups of citizens to gather according to their interests and make up the secondary associations that fill a robust civil society.

As time passed and the radical shifts in culture settled, these doctrines were muted by more "humanist" notions of the essential goodness of people, the inevitable progress of history, and the possibility of beneficent social cooperation. Alongside the evolution of democracy at this time, two other movements were shaping the Western world: the exponential advancement of science (which sometimes conflicted with religious understandings of how the world worked); and an emphasis on "objective" rationality, which is divorced from religious prejudices. This convergence of scientific and technological progress with human reason apart from any sort of divine

4. Taylor, *Secular Age*, 171.

influence created the space necessary for a secular framework to develop. These three streams—democracy, science, and "rationality"—came together at a unique time and would eventually grow into the Enlightenment project and the modern era. They also were the ink with which the promissory note of Secularism was written.

Secularism should not be confused with the secular. Secularism took the idea of the separation of church from the state and the decline of the central place of religion in society as markers toward the inevitability of the disappearance of religion altogether. The hope was that if we sanitize the public square by allowing only the "secular," then religion, the spiritual, the mysterious, and competing religious claims about moral good that were creating social conflict would fade into the background of history as a relic of pre-modern times. Much like the mythologies of ancient Greece and the early Roman Empire, religious worldviews like Christianity, Judaism, or Islam would be interesting fields of study but would have no real bearing on life in a modern world.

Richard Rorty captures the sentiment of secularism best when he argues for a kind of Jeffersonian compromise: guarantee religious liberty for the private lives of citizens—a source of psychological support for one's life during a time of transition—but remove religious reasons, religious language, and religious motivation from the public square because of the conflict that it causes.[5] For Rorty, if given enough time, democracy will produce a society "in which political action conducted in the name of religious belief is treated as a ladder up which our ancestors climbed, but one that now should be thrown away."[6] Taylor calls this idea of giving the secular enough time a "simple subtraction story"[7] about the inevitability of secularism that exchanges causation for correlation.

Rorty maintains his hope for secularism despite his rejection of the modern impulse toward "objective rationality and morality." In this, he is a hinge figure in the shift from the modern era to the postmodern era—especially in America. At its best, the postmodern project was an attempt to wrestle the definitions of "objective rationality" and "morality" away from the dominant voices in the West (Western European and American males) and recover rational and moral sentiments from those who have traditionally been at the margins. Postmodernity was, at first, a deconstructive

5. Rorty, *Philosophy and Social Hope*, 170–71.
6. Rorty, "Religion in the Public Square," 143.
7. Taylor, "Secular Age," 253.

project, demonstrating that "objectivity" is a difficult standard for human rationality and morality to carry: there is really no neutral vantage point that helps us settle disagreements over who is rational and what is moral. Subsequently, it was an attempt to recover the contribution of minority communities in the West and also non-Western perspectives. For Rorty, the nature of reality and the definition of truth are not something objectively "out there" to be discovered, but approximations of what works in different communal contexts. Therefore, as Rorty maintains, we have a lot to learn from communities that have been silenced throughout history because they have been on the underside of power. Rather than any kind of universal Truth, with a capital "T", Rorty argues for a truth (with a lowercase "t") that "is an expression of satisfaction at having found a solution to a problem."[8] This notion of non-universal truth relativizes truth to its social context and eliminates the need for an external frame of reference or for some kind of divine intervention or revelation to sustain social organization. The real possibility for hope and progress in society rests on human beings and their ability to pragmatically cooperate with one another in order to find solutions to important problems.

Rorty's version of epistemological pragmatism contests the idea that human beings have an external rational or moral standard that they must adjust their lives to and instead localizes rationality and morality in the shared agreements of a particular community.[9] The difficulty with a deconstructive project like this, however, is that it tends to double back on itself—you can only deconstruct for so long. And the promissory note of secularism is not outside of the reaches of the postmodern challenge itself. Is secularism just one more "-ism" in a long line ("imperialism," "colonialism," "rationalism," "scientism," "racism," and "triumphalism"), an overlay of the powerful onto the marginalized? And has it actually done the work that was promised? Has it reduced social conflict?

The lack of an external standard also raises difficult questions about how moral disagreements are settled between communities that share different understandings of the good, the true, and the beautiful. There are things that we want to say are universally wrong like slavery, the Holocaust, or the oppression of indigenous peoples, that seem to cross communal boundaries. Where do we go for shared understandings when communities

8. Rorty, *Achieving Our Country*, 29.
9. Rorty, *Philosophy and Social Hope*, 266–67.

disagree? Who gets to define the boundaries of a community in order to frame the important social agreements?

I am not saying that postmodernity was a vacant ideology—it had important corrective impulses that we need to carry forward—but that its strongest assets naturally lead us to something more. This "something more" seems to be reflected in recent studies on religion and spirituality. In research on the religious and spiritual lives of college students, the "National Study of Spirituality in Higher Education: Students' Search for Meaning and Purpose" chronicles the surprising resilience of "spirituality" in college students. Measured by five key "spiritual qualities"—(1) equanimity, (2) spiritual quest, (3) an ethic of caring, (4) charitable involvement, and (5) an ecumenical worldview—the study demonstrated that a student's spirituality actually increases during college. However, during that same time, their religious engagement decreases.[10] This reflects a parallel trend in a wider slice of American culture. According to the Pew Forum on Religion and Public Life, the fastest growing demographic in America is the "Nones"— those who do not choose to identify with a particular religious tradition but may still retain an interest in the spiritual.[11] According to Pew's research, the unaffiliated see religion as "too concerned with money and power, too focused on rules, and too involved in politics."[12] In a similar survey, but focused on Christianity, the Barna research group concluded that for people ranging in age from sixteen to twenty-nine, "One crucial insight kept popping up in our exploration. In studying thousands of outsiders' impressions, it is clear that Christians are primarily perceived for what they stand against. *We have become famous for what we oppose, rather than who we are for.*" When asked to characterize Christians, those surveyed described Christians as anti-homosexual, judgmental, hypocritical, and too political (as well as old-fashioned and boring).[13]

My interest in this book lies at the intersection of these narratives: the failure of secularism's promise, the waning of Postmodernity, the widening gap between increasing interest in the spiritual but decreasing identification with religion, and the possibilities for religion to contribute to the public good. There are different names for this intersection, including: post-Christian, post-postmodern, secular, and the age of authenticity. The

10. "Overall Findings," para. 3.

11. Pew Research Center, "'Nones' on the Rise."

12. Ibid.

13. Kinnaman and Lyons, *UnChristian*, 32.

efforts to name our experience in the early twenty-first century is a marker that another epochal shift is occurring. And I think that this shift might create room to renegotiate the boundaries of what kind of religious influence is acceptable in the public square.

If postmodernity challenged the notions of metanarratives because of the propensity to move those who do not have power to the margins of the conversation (history is written by the winners), postsecularity is trying to recover the idea that there is something larger than us. There is a mystery, an enchantment, and a spirituality that infuses human existence. To borrow a concept from Dietrich Bonheoffer, we are born in the middle.[14] That is, we find ourselves in a world that was already in motion; it began without us and will extend beyond us. And the uniquely human experience is to dare to make something out of this condition. What distinguishes postsecularity from postmodernity is the possibility of an external frame that we can access in our search for meaning and significance—trying to place our personal stories into a larger narrative that gives our random experiences a consistent thread of meaning. What distinguishes it from secularism is the acceptance and embrace of mystery, the reality of spiritual interest, and the hope of a diversified influence through cross-communal conversation.

There are also hints that, despite wariness toward and an unwillingness to identify with religion, the newly minted "Nones" still see a possibility for religion to be a positive force for social good. In a 2014 study, a Gallup Poll reported that almost 60 percent of Americans still think that religion can "answer today's problems." This number is trending downward (in 1957, 82 percent of Americans said that religion can "answer today's problems"); but the rates of decline are not commensurate with those who have discarded participation in formal religious practices.[15]

What do we make of these mixed messages? Spirituality is trending upward, and participation in formal religious traditions is moving downward. There is an increasing frustration that religious traditions are out of touch with reality, but still a hope that religion, at its best, can help answer some of today's most difficult questions. There is a wariness toward the particularity of religion, any "big story" that is absolutist in its commitments, but a recognition that there seems to be something beyond us. There is still the reality of religious violence in the world, but an idea that religious traditions should not be defined by their extreme edges. There is the belief

14. Bonhoeffer, *Christ the Center*, 61–64.
15. Newport, "Majority Still Says," 1.

that the separation of church and state is a virtuous principle in a pluralistic society, but countless examples of religious programs at the borders of that separation that are benefitting society. This tenuous space is what I want to call postsecularity. I am not alone in using this label as we search for ways to describe these shared experiences (Taylor and Jürgen Habermas are two scholars who have argued for the postsecular).[16] It's never easy to pinpoint when an actual shift in epochs occurs; we just often find ourselves swimming in different waters as cultural currents have taken us downstream a bit.

Let me give a cultural example that might locate this shift in the late twentieth century/early twenty-first century. Growing up as a child in the 1970s, I watched a Saturday morning cartoon called *Scooby-Doo*. Four young adults and one anthropomorphized dog were sleuths who helped solve "paranormal mysteries." They drove from place to place in a van with the words "Mystery Machine" emblazoned on the side. As each episode began, this group encountered some kind of monster or ghost who haunted a particular location. As the episode unfolded, these sleuths began to uncover clues to the identity of the villain. After several chase scenes and near-disastrous escapades, the show would culminate with a big reveal: the villain was not really a ghost or a monster after all, but a person who was using the fear of the paranormal to take advantage of someone else. This is the quintessential modern and secularist story: just give us enough time and we will figure out these apparent mysteries. In the early 2000s, when my children were old enough to watch cartoons, I stumbled upon the Scooby Doo movie, *Scooby-Doo and the Witch's Ghost*. And with a bit of nostalgia and pride I watched the program with them to demonstrate my sleuthing abilities and to try to figure out who the culprit was that was masquerading as a ghost. But to my surprise, the *Scooby-Doo* formula was turned on its head—the ghost was real. There are mysteries, there is something spiritual, and there might be something out there that is beyond the boundaries of science. Maybe *Scooby-Doo* marked the shift to postsecularity?

It is at this moment that I think we need to consider (or reconsider) the relationship between religion and democracy for a new era. How do we live our public and social lives as cultural tides shift? Is there any hope that religion might contribute positively to our communities as Western culture continues to pluralize? For the purposes of this book, I want to focus on a specific religion—Christianity. At the risk of narrowing the conversation

16. Taylor, *A Secular Age*; Habermas, "Notes on a Post-Secular Society."

too far, I will use evangelicalism as a representative of the Christian tradition for these few reasons: (1) Christianity has been the dominant religious tradition in the West, and for the past forty years evangelicals have seemed to be the dominant religious voice in the American political conversation; (2) I consider myself an evangelical in the broad sense—I have had an Augustine-like conversion experience as a young man and take the Hebrew and Christian Scriptures as authoritative for life and faith; (3) the religious right, especially white evangelical leaders, have received the bulk of attention in the media; and (4) this is my field of research as a scholar and intersects with my vocation as a Christian minister.

There are a lot of qualifications to be made by narrowing my focus. There are important lessons to be learned from ethnic-specific evangelical churches that I hope to hint at, but won't have space to give full treatment. The black church in America has had a different relationship to democracy than white evangelicals. I also think that it is interesting and increasingly important to consider Islam's relationship to democracy. We can also learn something from Judaism's role in Western democracies. I stumbled across a quotation in Michael Walzer's book *The Revolution of the Saints: A Study in the Origins of Radical Politics* that animates the aims of this book. And as you will see in later chapters, there is an important metaphor that was borrowed from Judaism that has obscured the relationship between Christian faith and Western democracy since democracy's nascent stages in the seventeenth century.[17]

So where to go from here? In chapter 1, "Independence and the Art of Pluralism," I will argue that there is a science and an art in how to set the boundaries between religion and government. The science is in what we traditionally call "the separation of church and state" in both of its meanings: not allowing the state to coerce citizens in their particular religious commitments and not allowing particular religious communities to coerce citizens toward their legislative goals. Maintaining some semblance of these harder edges is increasingly important as pluralism increases in the West. The art is in the blur of activity between those two boundaries. In chapter 2, "Images of Exile," I try to articulate how a borrowed metaphor from the Hebrew Scriptures captured the imagination of the Puritans and set America on a trajectory that equated nationalism with Christian faithfulness. I argue that the New Testament writers borrow a different metaphor from Jewish

---

17. For a more detailed analysis of the contribution of Christianity—especially Calvinism—in the formation of democratic ideals, see Walzer, *The Revolution of the Saints*.

political life—the image of exile—to encourage their readers in the way to follow Jesus in their public lives.

With these two frameworks in place, I then set out to show that a dynamic, tension-filled relationship between the Christian tradition and the democratic tradition help one another flourish. In chapter 3, I maintain that, by its very nature, democracy needs a complementary tradition. Its virtues of accommodating a variety of different and polyphonic voices in the public square and its principle of harm as its defining baseline ethic need more substantial virtues to help carry it forward. Christianity's Royal Law (Matt 7:12), its attention to the poor and marginalized (Jas 2:1–26), and Jesus' model of servanthood (Mark 10:42–46) are important pillars that can help prop up core democratic principles. In chapter 4, I argue that the Christian church has needed democracy and its thin ethic of harm as a prophetic voice at the edges of Christendom. Christianity has been the dominant tradition in the West, and when a group has power, it tends to lean toward conservatism to maintain its influence for the good it aims for. As various groups have argued for more rights, this has challenged the Christian tradition toward a more faithful expression of itself. In chapter 5, I will bring these two complements together in prophetic tension—opening up the public square to religious language, religious reasons, and religious commitments in order to draw the best out of both traditions.

Finally, in chapter 6, I will recount some "Experiments of Exile." There is a model in the Jewish tradition for what it means to be in exile—to use your natural gifts and abilities in cooperation and faithfulness to God so that your neighbors flourish. There are myriad examples of this happening, and they often are not reported or are overshadowed. My hope is to capture a few of these experiments to demonstrate that the Christian tradition at its best is creative and caring, and that the democratic tradition benefits from these supererogatory virtues.

1

Independence and the Art of Pluralism

THE DEFINING QUESTION OF the post-secular is: "What do we do with religion?" Obviously, the spiritual is meaningful in many people's lives, and as I alluded to in the introduction, it is surprisingly resistant to the "simple subtraction story" of secularism. Maybe "spiritual" is just ambiguous enough to fit within Rorty's boundaries of the Jeffersonian compromise. Certainly, a case could be made for the privatization of spirituality over against the public nature of religion. A person's spirituality can be an isolated and very individual exercise for personal and emotional fulfillment. Religion, however, is by nature communal, and therefore public.

Here, I want to avoid any precise definitions of "spiritual" or "religious," so as not to obscure our intuitions about these things. Rather, let's just work with the spiritual as a set of beliefs and practices that bring personal meaning and significance. Two people can consider themselves spiritual, but not share any beliefs or practices. Religion differs in this way: two people who call themselves a member of a particular religion (Buddhism, Christianity, Hinduism, Islam, Judaism, etc.) will share some common beliefs and practices. This sharing puts a community of people in relationship with one another and in relationship to those that do not share those same commitments.

As a public phenomenon, then, religion becomes a part of the conversation of social organization: How do we bring people together in a way that everyone can flourish? Can different religions co-exist together and in the same space with the non-religious? I want to be careful not to assume or affirm the late twentieth-century drift toward putting all religious traditions on the same mountain and washing out their distinctiveness. To do this says something about the nature of god (I'll use lowercase "g" to be all-inclusive), about religious practice, and about the good, the true, and the beautiful. I am not affirming nor denying the veracity of this religious idea, just that it relativizes and minimizes long-standing religious traditions. Scotty McLennan argues that this mountain theology *humanizes* those traditions by putting them on a common quest.[1] But my concern here is to treat different religions on their own terms (and in this book, specifically Christianity) and negotiate what that means in our common public space.

Quoting an unknown predecessor, Winston Churchill famously said, "Democracy is the worst form of government, except for all those other forms that have been tried from time to time."[2] Democracy is a way of social organization that purports to bring all citizens into the public space to negotiate the requisite conditions for life together. Embedded in that invitation is the possibility (inevitability?) of conflict over competing visions of what a good life together might look like. These are often settled by utilitarian calculations of the most good for the most people affirmed by a majority of citizens. Religious citizens are invited into that process, but there is a characteristic difficulty in their participation. Religious traditions, because they are anchored in something outside of human authority (Taylor's "external frame"), are absolutist in nature and somewhat uncompromising on their vision of what it means to live the good life. Their reasons and actions are sometimes foreign to those who are not religious or for those from a different religious tradition. Democracy, in contrast, is contingent, tethered to the information available at the moment, compromising, subject to rapid change of opinion, and does its best to make its processes and conclusions available to all people.

Negotiating the relationship between democracy and Christianity can get twisted quickly. To be sure, there are shared agreements between the religious and non-religious that easily find consensus; but the public square can be a raucous environment. If the university is the institution where competing ideas and ideologies are supposed to be treated civilly and with respect, the public square can sometimes be harsh, dismissive, and demanding. If postmodernity taught us anything, it is that we most often judge another's moral or rational framework through our own particular

---

1. See McLennan's book *Finding Your Religion* for a broadly inclusive argument for this view, and *Jesus Was a Liberal* for a more specific application to Christianity.

2. House of Commons Speech, November 11, 1947. "Parliament Bill (Hansard, 11 November 1947)." Churchill, *Churchill by Himself*, 573.

experiences. This should breed caution and humility in our judgments of others' ideas, but those are not the core virtues in the rapid pace of political conversations. Eloquence can win out over reasonableness and rationality, and charisma can carry an argument farther than content. The pace in the public square can sometimes lead to the mistaken notion that there seem to be important shared agreements—we are marching in the same parade—when in fact we are working with different definitions of important ideas but have failed to clarify what we mean.[3] It is important to stop, step back, and consider the way that our own traditions shade our lenses.

I have used the word "tradition," and I am utilizing it in a technical sense, because I think that it is a helpful philosophical concept when we talk about the boundaries between religion and politics. Alasdair MacIntyre argued that the failure of the Enlightenment impulse to define moral and rational boundaries universally—for all times, in all cultures, and irrespective of differences in perspectives—did not produce the kind of moral progress that was promised. It was difficult to define a constitutive good that could gather the complexities of our moral life together in a coherent way that everyone could agree upon. While much good was achieved, the failure of this project put the possibility of sharing a common moral framework and common moral language in jeopardy, while at the same time fostering a pessimism toward any view that would define a good for "someone else."

If we truly are in a post-secular age, then even our most basic efforts at finding something common or neutral in our moral understandings (neutralizing the public square) are conditioned by our communal sympathies and definitions of "neutral." MacIntyre calls this stage three of Western culture's moral decline.[4] Stage one, for MacIntyre, was grounding moral principles and practices in something objective—something "out there"—that guided human behavior. Stage two was the rejection of an objective standard in favor of a uniquely human standard (e.g., reason, utility, the categorical imperative, choice, etc.), and stage three, as noted, was the unsettled character of our public debates and the "apparent arbitrariness" of each of the parties.[5] Facing this crisis, MacIntyre thinks that we have two options: (1) we could embrace the Nietzschean perspective and assert our moral positions through power, politics, and law, or (2) we could revisit the idea of a *telos*—a purpose for humanity—and its consequent moral

3. Walzer, *Thick and Thin*, 3.

4. MacIntyre, *After Virtue*, 19.

5. Ibid., 256.

companion—the virtue tradition. By "the moral decline of Western culture," MacIntyre is not referring to the advances made in human rights for those who have been habitually on the underside of power in the West, but how morality has devolved into the embrace of Nietzsche in the assertion of power.

James Davison Hunter argues that the church did not break stride with this Nietzschean impulse and traded in the ethic of Jesus for a stake in power politics and working toward establishing (re-establishing?) a moral vision of the kingdom of God through legislation—especially in America. For Hunter, this attempt at "changing the world" through politics did not accomplish as much as was hoped for and buried the good news of the gospel of Christ under party platforms. The gospel is sometimes indistinguishable from affirmations of specific political ideologies. In lamenting the increasingly negative perception of the Christian church in American culture, Hunter says that "Christians should remain silent for a season, until we can learn how to talk about politics in a non-Nietzschean manner."[6] For Hunter, the church is no different than the world in its attempts to control the moral future through power, and thus ironically has lost its moral influence. It has contributed as one of the voices among the many who are trying to tell their story amidst a moral horizon with as many possibilities as there are distinct communities. But we are left with the same dilemma: "How do we negotiate our lives together? And how do we span the chasm between a particular community's notion of the good and any sense of universal moral obligation?" This is probably the most commonly perplexing question in the field of ethics. It seems that MacIntyre's argument about the moral decline of Western culture is that Nietzsche will always trap us on the particularist side of "Lessing's Ditch," and the only way forward to a moral consensus is through accumulating as much power as possible.

MacIntyre's project in several of his books is to try to articulate a different path. He wants to recover the idea of a *telos* and the concept of virtue in order to answer these important questions in a meaningful way. I am not as concerned about his conclusion that a Thomistic Aristotelian Catholic tradition is the most rational tradition; rather, I want to focus on MacIntyre's broad definition of a "tradition" as a foundation for how to move forward in negotiating the relationship between religion and democracy. If we add some texture to this concept, I think that it can do some real work in how to negotiate our public space.

6. Hunter, *To Change the World*, 186.

MacIntyre argues that the Enlightenment project of unhinging rationality and morality from its particular communal formulations was misguided and ultimately impossible: "[m]orality which is no particular society's morality is to be found nowhere."[7] Consequently, we need to recover the starting point that competing moral traditions develop out of particular communities (the thesis of postmodernity). MacIntyre wants to start communally, but then give an account of how to adjudicate between these competing moral claims, and a *tradition* does that work for him. He begins with a simple definition: a tradition is "an argument extended through time in which certain fundamental agreements are defined and redefined in terms of two kinds of conflict."[8] The first kind of conflict is an external conflict in which a central belief (or first principle) of a tradition is challenged from an outside source. For example, Charles Darwin's *On the Origin of Species* was an external challenge to Christianity's interpretation of the first few chapters of Genesis in the late nineteenth century. The second kind of conflict is an internal conflict in which a central belief is challenged from within the particular tradition. Martin Luther's Ninety-Five Theses, which kickstarted the Protestant Reformation, is an example of an internal conflict. A successful or robust tradition is one that is able to survive and thrive among these conflicts.

While MacIntyre seems to advocate a somewhat Marxian dialectic and adversarial posture in his definition of a tradition, we can also take this to be a more benign historical process—understanding a tradition is to know something of its history and how it has developed into what it is today. Thus, a tradition is a kind of narrative that tells a particular story of the development of understanding about several key features of human existence: what is real, what is true, what is human nature, what is good, what is ultimately important, and how we can know these things. For MacIntyre, a tradition develops in three stages (he likes three stages). First, a tradition begins contingently with the assertion of a belief or a set of beliefs by an authority. These initial beliefs are often connected to an authoritative (sacred) text, and commonly go unquestioned in their early development. Second, inadequacies in the initial beliefs, texts, or authorities begin to surface through internal or external epistemological challenges. Finally, a tradition matures as responses to those inadequacies are formulated. As a tradition progresses through these stages, a form of inquiry develops and

7. Ibid., 277.

8. MacIntyre, *Whose Justice? Which Rationality?*, 12.

practices are institutionalized that define the tradition's account of rationality and morality. So it is possible within any large-scale tradition to develop subtraditions over time that challenge one or more aspects of the institutionalized form of inquiry.[9] It is important to note here two caveats to this definition of a tradition: (1) a healthy tradition welcomes both internal and external questions as a way to strengthen itself. And (2) fundamentalism in any tradition is an unwillingness to look at the questions being raised in fear that the tradition might fail to answer those questions and ultimately stagnate or die. Richard Rorty calls this kind of fundamentalism "conversation stoppers,"[10] because you cannot really move forward in a conversation if someone is not willing to examine his or her assumptions and beliefs.

Because a tradition starts historically and contingently, MacIntyre can affirm Rorty's idea that there are no capital-T truths. Any belief or first principle can be shown to be false at a moment in history. However, MacIntyre does not want to lock truth inside a particular community's understanding. He holds a "modest" universalism that starts from the ground up, not the top down—as a tradition develops and matures over time, its truths (with lowercase "t's") become larger—that is, they have stood the test of time, and therefore our epistemological confidence in the truth of these principles is higher. So MacIntyre wants to affirm that rational and moral principles develop out of communities (the postmodern impulse), and that there are no capital-T truths (because we cannot rule out the possibility that future experience may demonstrate a belief or a set of beliefs to be inadequate), but he wants to steer truth out into the open conversation where traditions might come into conversation and conflict.[11] He argues that some traditions will be shown to have better resources to emerge from those kinds of conflicts than others.[12]

Accordingly, for a belief to be false, one has to be able to look back at a tradition's beliefs, texts, and authorities and say that these no longer account for reality (our lived experience) and therefore had to be changed. Accounting for reality is the mind's ability to form expectations based on experience and activity that do not disappoint us; and to be able to "retain and recover" through memory what it has encountered.[13]

9. Ibid., 355–59.
10. Rorty, "Religion in the Public Square," 143.
11. MacIntyre, *Whose Justice? Which Rationality?*, 361.
12. Ibid., 364.
13. Ibid., 356.

MacIntyre's notion of a tradition starts contingently, and is thus relatively true, based on a particular community's practices of reason and their experience of how those practices match reality. Because different traditions have unique starting points and are at various stages of maturity, they may contradict one another and still be considered rational in this understanding of truth. At this point, MacIntyre argues that conversation and reality draw us out of the confines of our community and into the public space where ideas interact. When this happens, we can look for instances of lowercase-t truths that can cross communities. There are two ways that this happens: First, when a tradition bumps its head against reality in a way that we can no longer trust our expectations; this creates a disequilibration in the coherence and consistency of a tradition and sends its adherents back to its beliefs, texts, and authorities. At this point, another tradition may account for that specific reality better and have more explanatory power—it can be shown to be superior. Second, when two traditions are in conversation, commonalities may surface that both communities affirm—a notion of reiterative truth. Reiterative truth is a truth or a set of truths that different communities share.

In his book *Interpretation and Social Criticism*, Michael Walzer argues that, when you spot instances of shared beliefs or moral understandings across traditions, it is a marker of truths that are universally true. Conversely, if there are acts or beliefs that "shock the conscience," and other communities have the same response of moral indignation or condemnation, it is also a marker of something that we might consider universally morally wrong. So there are positive and negative first principles of traditions that seem to cross particularist understandings. For Walzer, the more instances a truth or moral formulation is manifested across cultures and communities, the more we can be confident that it is universally true.[14] And correspondingly, if the number of different cultures that express moral indignation against a particular act is great, we can be more confident that it is false.

Here, an example might help illustrate MacIntyre's notion of how a tradition might move toward capital-T Truth in conversation and conflict. He argues that the Ptolemaic and Copernican astronomies of the late-sixteenth and early-seventeenth centuries were in an epistemological crisis—unable to account for reality. What Galileo did by arguing for a heliocentric universe was reframe astronomy so that the internal inconsistencies of

14. Walzer, *Interpretation and Social Criticism*.

medieval understandings of the universe could be understood and completed with Galileo's new conception.[15] MacIntyre appeals to this kind of case study because there are concrete examples in the history of science that help minimize ambiguity: there are clear examples of research programs that have been shown to be superior in their ability to account for reality. This example also crosses over into an important theological crisis. Galileo challenged the geo-centric theology of his day. This put the interpretation of the first chapters of Genesis at the center of this epistemological challenge. This new understanding of cosmology helped frame a reinterpretation of the Hebrew Scriptures, and therefore provided a more coherent narrative of Genesis. This process created new possibilities for an orthodox interpretation of the Hebrew Scriptures and helped Christianity reframe its understanding of biblical interpretation.

Why all this epistemological wrangling over truth, relativism, practices of reason, and accounting for reality? How does this relate to my opening question of "What do we do with religion in public?" In various iterations, scholars have been working on the same epistemological question: "How do we avert the moral triumphalism and colonialism of both Western Christendom and its sibling, the Secular Enlightenment Project, without devolving into radical relativism?" Also, "What does this mean for the possibility of moral knowledge?"

Nation-states that work to accommodate a pluralistic public square through democracy inherently create conversation and disagreement. The question is then, "Do we have any resources to adjudicate between competing claims about what is good, what is true, and what is real in this environment?" And, "What kind of role can religion play?" I have tried to lay out a brief summary of MacIntyre's notion of a tradition because it seems to fit the sensibilities of our post-secular age—it recovers the historical and communal moorings of moral knowledge, but it does not trap moral knowledge behind radical relativism. So I want to put the liberal (and I am using "liberal" in the most generous, non-politicized manner—the inclusive democratic tradition) and the Christian tradition into conversation together to chart a way forward in understanding the relationship between the church and the state in contemporary American politics.

Unlike its European counterparts, the nascent democratic tradition in America began with some room to be creative (almost all Democracies have sordid beginnings that often came about through violent means;

---

15. MacIntyre, *Three Rival Versions*, 157–58.

and the American experiment was no exception). It had its religious influences—especially a Puritan hope to escape the tyranny of subjugation in England for a new "promised land"—and its discordant Enlightenment inspiration that envisioned social cooperation free of religious coercion. As plurality increased, the disentangling of Christianity from democracy became necessary. Moreover, as the influence of Christianity waned in the West, more emphasis was placed on separating Christianity from its undue legislative influence in favor of a more inclusive system. Now, as pluralism continues to increase, a new problem is occurring—everyone feels marginalized. McLennan has argued that the once influential liberal Christian movement has been pushed to the margins by the "religious right" and "secularists."[16] The burgeoning group of "new atheists" (Richard Dawkins, Sam Harris, Christopher Hitchens, et al.) have decried their own marginalization by the "religious," and a chorus of evangelicals have mourned the loss of a "Christian America" and blamed the "liberals" and "secularists."[17]

The liberal democratic tradition is unique in its ability to handle this increasing plurality. Its authoritative texts (minimally the Declaration of Independence, Bill of Rights, and Constitution) guaranteed that every citizen will be protected from undue harm and has the freedom to pursue their own life plan within certain minimal boundary conditions: that they do not harm others along the way and that they fulfill their obligations to society—life, liberty, and the pursuit of happiness. Politics is the means to manage social organization when competing life plans come into conflict.[18] Through the practices of giving and receiving reasons in public, electing representatives, and balancing the power between the three branches of government we hope to give the most people the greatest opportunities to pursue their aspirations.

Ideally, democracy allows citizens (and those non-citizens that contribute to a nation's health) to determine the constituent goods of society and how those goods get distributed justly. Walzer argues that we use three criteria for determining goods and their distribution: need, desert, and free exchange. What does every citizen need to flourish, what do certain citizens deserve in order to flourish, and what space can we create to accommodate different interests through free exchange. He fiddles a bit with the Declaration of Independence's "life, liberty, and the pursuit of happiness" by

16. McLennan, *Jesus Was a Liberal*, vii.

17. Hynes, *In Defense of the Religious Right*, x.

18. Walzer, *In God's Shadow*, 66.

arguing for three goods that all person's need: protection of life, the ability to pursue one's own life plan within the boundaries of not harming others, and membership in community.[19]

Inherent in democracy's strength of accommodating variegated and diverse communities are at least four weaknesses: (1) the liberal democratic tradition will always marginalize some citizens—utilitarian calculations of the good means that there will be a minority of citizens whose good goes undistributed; (2) it is difficult to make positive claims about the direction of "society" without common moral assumptions and language; (3) in its practice of giving and receiving reasons, the liberal democratic tradition creates conflict but does not have a mechanism to resolve that conflict except for the power of coercion, and finally; (4) it can create a tyranny of the majority—where the majority is morally wrong, but has the power. A clear example of this last weakness was the American eugenics movement that took place in the early twentieth century and fostered sterilization laws to help "strengthen society." I will say more about this in a later chapter.

It is precisely at the intersection of democracy's strengths and weaknesses that the role of religious sentiment and practice is negotiated. And this negotiation is an art. Historically, this relationship has had varied instantiations. I have already mentioned two: the protection of religious freedom (within limits) given in the First Amendment to the Constitution. "Congress shall make no law respecting an establishment of religion, or prohibiting the free exercise thereof; or abridging the freedom of speech, or of the press; or the right of the people peaceably to assemble, and to petition the Government for a redress of grievances." And as for the protection of government from religious coercion, there is Thomas Jefferson's famous "wall of separation" that was supposed to separate church and state.[20] These two notions of separation—government cannot establish a particular religion, and the religious have no coercive power in legislation—form the hard edges of the boundaries between the Christian tradition and the democratic tradition in America. It is important to note here that this is a uniquely American exemplification of these edges. In Great Britain and France, these boundaries are negotiated differently, as are the borders between Islam and democracy in some of the nation-states in the Middle East.

But I am concerned here about the boundaries between the Christian tradition and the democratic tradition in America as an example that can

19. Walzer, *Spheres of Justice*, 31.
20. "Jefferson's Wall of Separation Letter."

be analogized and applied in different circumstances. If I can make a case that the most interesting aspects of the relationship between Christianity and democracy in America is between the hard edges of separation and their distinct meanings, this creates artistic space for other religious traditions and other models of democracy to navigate these tricky questions. The lines of separation frame the boundaries to begin painting the art on the canvas. But I want to argue that, inside those boundaries, there is much more room for creativity and intersection in the relationship between religion and democracy.[21] The lines of demarcation create the independence necessary to distinguish the core aspects of each tradition, but the art inside the frame is what is most interesting. And like most great paintings, you cannot make out the picture from the blur of the first few brushstrokes.

It is important to mention a few representative scholars in this conversation who use something like MacIntyre's notion of a tradition to argue for the purity and integrity of their respective traditions. They work to provide the outer boundaries to mark out how each tradition can remain independent and avoid what they see as the "corrupting influence" of the other.

The secular move to create a public space free of religious coercion has received the lion's share of attention since the cultural revolution of the 1960s. The removal of prayer from schools (1962) and the removal of the Ten Commandments from public buildings (2005) are just two examples of the continued press to free the public square from undue religious influence and control. And, scholars have argued that if you take democracy and treat it as a tradition, it can stand on its own without religion.

Richard Rorty, Jeff Stout, and Mark Claddis are three out of many scholars who argue for a robust democratic tradition. Rorty goes to extreme lengths to argue that the citizens of a democracy are better off if religion is sequestered into private enclaves and kept away from the democratic process. He argues that an unadulterated democratic tradition is one where civil society constantly widens to include more and more possibilities for human happiness for as many people as possible. He emphasizes the moral progress of the secularizing trajectory of the democratic project in America and tells the story of how unhinging traditional epistemological, moral, and anthropological concepts from religious belief has contributed to that progress. The heroes of Rorty's narrative are Walt Whitman, William James, John Dewey, and Charles Darwin. For Rorty, historical reflection replaced theological motivation for social life; society has progressed

21. Cladis, "Painting Landscapes of Religion."

through the necessary stages so that God is no longer necessary to intervene in human history to set things right—human beings hold the hope for progress in society. William James and John Dewey spoke of democracy as a kind of religion unto itself, and they used religious and poetic overtones to describe it: "[Democracy] is a kind of religion, and we are bound not to admit its failure. . . . It is neither a form of government nor a social expediency, but a metaphysic of the relation of man and his experience in nature."[22] The democratic tradition is often infused with poetic sentiment, eschatological lilt, and metaphysical allusions as a secular alternative to the gap created by removing religion from the public conversation. Rorty sees the contribution of religious voices in opposition to slavery, in the positive gains of the Civil Rights Movement, and in liberation theology as constructive moments in which religion contributed to moral progress. They were not, however, necessary conditions for that progress. Eventually, democracy would have gotten there on its own; and Rorty maintains that for every Martin Luther King Jr., there is a Jerry Falwell or Pat Robertson that seem to work toward undoing the moral gains that have been accomplished. Because of his hope in the democratic tradition, Rorty is willing to sacrifice the Martin Luther King Jrs. of the world to prevent the harm he sees in the Moral Majority or the Christian Coalition. He is on the extreme end of the democratic tradition, but he has many sympathizers. He argues that the religious make bad citizens because they have allegiances outside of their fellow human beings.[23]

He objects to the religious impulse to define the good life by an objective standard outside of human consensus. He opposes the divided loyalties of the religious who do not give wholehearted devotion to democracy. And he disdains the harm done to citizens in the name of religion.

Jeffrey Stout is more measured in his argument that the democratic tradition can stand on its own. He takes MacIntyre's terms of a tradition and argues for a robust democratic tradition that can tolerate and accommodate religion as a positive force for good in society. Before Stout added texture to his notion of a democratic tradition with his book, *Blessed are the Organized*, which included the role of religion in providing cultural architecture for supporting democracy, he borrowed Jean Bethke Elshtain's image of a stream as a metaphor for "the sources of ethical and religious

---

22. Rorty, *Achieving Our Country*, 9.
23. Fortanet and Rosato, "Pragmatism and Democracy," 419.

virtue that sustain our democracy."[24] Elshtain was arguing that democracy may end up draining the tributaries that support it, but Stout wants to counter that argument with poetic sentiment from Walt Whitman—that Elshtain has asked the wrong question. Instead of asking what supports democracy (focusing on the tributaries that feed it), we should be asking where democracy is going, appreciating its historical currents for what it has produced. For Stout, if one stays faithful to the minimal practices of giving and receiving reasons, democracy will continue to produce positive fruit. Stout's metaphor is reminiscent of imagery used from Psalm 1 in the Hebrew Bible: "Blessed is the person . . . they will be like trees planted by streams of water, which yield its fruit in season" (Ps 1a, 3a–b).[25] Both Stout and Rorty want to add layers of meaning to the democratic tradition and Stout, in contrast to Rorty, has a place for religion in general and Christianity in particular that can be accommodated by the democratic tradition.

Stanley Hauerwas is Rorty's Christian doppleganger. Hauerwas wants to free Christianity from the corrupting influence of the democratic tradition. For Hauerwas, any blurring of the lines of distinction between the church and state washes out the distinctiveness of the church's beliefs, virtues, and practices. He argues that the grasp for cultural acceptance and political power, which started in the fourth century CE, has actually backfired on the church; playing by the new rules of any dominant culture has deleterious consequences for both the church and larger culture. Here there are echoes of Hunter's argument. For Hauerwas, the very nature of Rorty's Jeffersonian compromise is a loss for the Christian church because it separates belief from practice, which privatizes religion and subordinates it to the government.[26] For Hauerwas, the Jeffersonian compromise is just a small part in a larger compromise that began with Constantine, caught steam during the Enlightenment, and continues to run forward in our understanding of the religious right and organizations like the Moral Majority or the Christian Coalition. Hauerwas argues that when the church seeks affirmation or accommodation by the wider culture, it ultimately thins out the distinctiveness of a Christian ethic in a way that deeply held Christian principles like "love" and "justice" lose their substantive meaning.

---

24. Stout, *Democracy and Tradition*; Stout, *Blessed Are the Organized*.

25. Unless otherwise indicated, all Scripture references in this book are from the NRSV.

26. Hauerwas, *In Good Company*, 200.

Hauerwas is equally as critical of the Enlightenment project as Rorty. The attempt to ground reason and morality apart from anything objectively "out there" moved morality inward, thus undermining the entire project altogether: "Ironically, since the Enlightenment's triumph, people no longer kill one another in the name of God but in the name of nation-states."[27] For Hauerwas, washed-out language, privatized belief, and continued conflict in society have created a vacuum that only a substantive Christian tradition can fill. So he has hope that a renewed, vibrant, and uncompromised Christianity can demonstrate to the world what a flourishing life in the kingdom of God looks like. He defines the mission of the church and the role of Christianity in culture in this way: "I argue [that] the church's social task is first of all its willingness to be a community formed by a language that the world does not share."[28] The church is to be "nothing less than . . . a community capable of hearing the story of God we find in the scripture and living in a manner that is faithful to this story."[29] This is the best hope for the world.

Hauerwas refuses to be labeled a sectarian and is careful to avoid language of "withdrawal" from culture. He eschews H. Richard Niebuhr's well-known typology of five Christian responses to culture (see Niebuhr, *Christ and Culture*) in favor of John Howard Yoder's typology: activist, conversionist, and confessing churches. If Hauerwas is Rorty's Christian parallel, Yoder is Stout's. They share similar concerns as they contend for their respective traditions. Yoder argues for the uniqueness of the Christian tradition and the necessity of maintaining a distinction between it and any form of government. But he also creates some room for the blur as these two traditions intersect. The aim of his writings is to recover the apostolic vision of the political relevance of Jesus from the disastrous effects of the fourth-century "Constantinian compromise."[30] Yoder's Constantinian compromise was the wedding of the church with the Roman Empire in a way that confused the *telos* of the church with the state and produced some of the negative examples (Crusades, Spanish Inquisition, etc.) that Rorty picks up to argue for the Jeffersonian compromise. Yoder sees in the pages of the New Testament a thick Jesus who offers a distinct social ethic for our concrete, particular, and contemporary moral choices. The axis of this

27. Hauerwas, *After Christendom?*, 27.

28. Hauerwas, *Against the Nations*, 11.

29. Hauerwas, *Community of Character*, 1.

30. Yoder, *Priestly Kingdom*, 129.

social ethic is the forming of a distinct people—"the paradigm of people-hood that bridges the gulf between an individual follower of Jesus and the social structures of the world."[31]

For Yoder, this believing community should be understood as a political entity in the simplest meaning of the term.[32] He argues that we should not create a false dichotomy between faith and politics.

> Politics affirms an unblinking recognition that we deal with mat-ters of power, of rank and of money, of costly decisions and dirty hands, of memories and feelings. The difference between church and state, of between a faithful and an unfaithful church is not that one is political and the other is not, but that they are political in different ways.[33]

Thus, for Yoder, the Christian church must recover from the muddled so-cial ethic that resulted in the strange amalgamation of church with state and recapture its distinctiveness as a community who lives out the witness of Christ to the world.

This coincides in many ways with the work of Hauerwas, but Yoder makes an important distinction. Instead of the community standing in con-trast to the world, Yoder argues that the church is to be something positive *for* the world.[34] You can see this in the titles of Hauerwas's book and Yoder's counter: *Against the Nations* and *For the Nations* respectively. Yoder finds an illustration of this kind of positive modeling presence in God's admoni-tion to the Jewish exiles in Babylon, [to] "seek the welfare of the city where I have sent you into exile, and pray to the LORD on its behalf, for in its welfare you will find your welfare" (Jer 29:7). There will be more to say about exile in a later chapter, but here he argues that the church is a paradigm (a model to be adopted) and a prophet (speaking to the world about the beauty and grace of the kingdom of God). In the church's prophetic role, it can affirm the practices of the world that reflect the values and virtues of the kingdom of God—albeit imperfectly.

Let me sum up my argument so far. What I have tried to do in this chapter is to begin to mark out the boundaries of the Christian tradition and the liberal democratic tradition to create space for each tradition to flourish on its own terms. I have argued that the definitive boundaries

31. Yoder, *For the Nations*, 218, 185.
32. Yoder, *Christian Witness*, viii.
33. Ibid., ix.
34. Yoder, *For the Nations*, 6.

between church and state (the science of independence) frame the canvas for an art to take place. This frame must be there to preserve each tradition's integrity. I have mentioned Richard Rorty and Stanley Hauerwas as scholars who want to argue for the purity of their tradition because of the compromise they see when each tradition crosses the line of independence. They are scholars who are concerned with the frame.

I have also included Jeffrey Stout and John Yoder, who want to blur the edges of the canvas to make room for the positive contribution of each tradition to the other—they paint near the boundaries of the frame. Specifically, they are trying to smooth out some of the hard edges of Rorty's and Hauerwas's views respectively without abandoning their important criticisms. They want to make some creative space to see what kind of good the "other" can offer.

In this, I have used Alasdair MacIntyre's definition of a tradition: a narrative that extends through time, telling a particular story about several key features of human existence: what is real, what is true, what is human nature, what is good, what is ultimately important, and how we can know these things. I think that this is a helpful way to honor our intuitions about reason, morality, and moral formation—that they begin communally, but are not trapped behind communal walls. It is also a way to talk about these two great traditions (Christianity and democracy) that honors the integrity of each and helps us negotiate what kind of relationship that they might have in the future.

2

Images of Exile

Borrowing Jewish Images for Christian Political Praxis

WHEN A TRAIN COMES to a stop in Great Britain, the conductor always says, "Mind the gap." The gap is the distance between the train and the platform. Each gap is a different size, and if you aren't paying attention as you step off the train, you might trip. In this chapter, I want to mind another gap. I have already argued that a post-secular age is defined by the gap described by the "Nones" that are taking up spirituality, but do not want to identify themselves with formal religion. They may syncretistically use religious practices from different religious traditions as a way to enhance their spiritual lives, but it is a borrowing and not an owning of those practices. The gap that I want to focus on in this chapter is the gap between people's perception of Jesus as a religious figure and their perception of Christianity as a religious tradition. This is more of an anecdotal gap anchored in my experience as a campus minister, but it has some quantitative support. First, the anecdote: I mentioned in the introduction that my conversations as a campus minister at Stanford are mostly with people who hold a neutral or positive view of Jesus as a religious figure. They appreciate his teachings on love, humility, peace, and justice. But when it comes to Christianity as a religious tradition, their perception is negative—they associate Christianity with judgmentalism, authoritarianism, pride, conflict, and partiality.

This is supported in Dave Kinnaman and Gabe Lyons's findings in *UnChristian*. When they surveyed millennials in 2008, those who considered themselves outsiders to the faith thought of Christians as "anti-homosexual (91 percent), judgmental (87 percent), and hypocritical (85 percent)."[1] Lyons and Kinnaman concluded these findings by saying, "One crucial insight kept popping up in our exploration. In studying thousands of outsiders' impressions, it is clear that Christians are primarily perceived for what they stand against. *We have become famous for what we oppose, rather than who we are for.*"[2]

How did the church get to the point where Christianity as a tradition and Christians in particular are often looked at with derision and as an anchor around the neck of society rather than a cool breeze blowing into its sails? Christians, especially those we commonly refer to as evangelicals, seem to be like an old boyfriend or girlfriend continually hanging around asking Western culture to re-consider getting back together. Is there a way to "mind the gap" between the perception of Jesus and the perception surrounding those that are considered his followers?

It would be easy to answer that this is just a "perceived problem," and the church needs more public relations consultants; in chapter 6 I will try to recover some of the beautiful things that the Christian church has done as models in the negotiation of the boundaries between church and state. But for now, the gap is real and must be addressed. There is a history for my defining question: "Is this a time where the relationship between religion (and especially Christianity) and democracy in America needs to be renegotiated?" And with the current perception of Christianity, especially evangelical Christianity, in the public consciousness, the answer to that defining question will be "no." Is this just how the Christian tradition is and should be understood, or is this one of MacIntyre's epistemological crises that might help reframe one or more of Christianity's beliefs, texts, or authorities so that it can posture itself differently?

The American story is littered with religious symbols, rhetoric, charismatic figures, and relics. All of these have taken on an aura of "magic"—a kind of power incommensurate to the actual thing itself—that has become a mythology. Because Christianity has been the dominant religious tradition in the West, and certainly in America, this is primarily a Christian mythology, with a smattering of providential deism, Unitarian Universalism, friendly secularism, and militant atheism to stir the pot. Richard Hughes argues that this mythology is tied to six beliefs: (1) the myth of a chosen nation, (2) the myth of nature's nation, (3) the myth of the Christian nation, (4) the myth of the millennial nation, (5) the mythic dimensions of

1. Kinnaman and Lyons, *UnChristian,* 27.
2. Ibid., 26. Emphasis in original.

capitalism, and (6) the myth of an innocent nation.[3] These six beliefs (not an exhaustive list) are the watermarks in the background that shade the way we look at our cultural landscape—sometimes apparent, but always present. Two of these beliefs are especially important for my purposes: the belief that America is/was a "chosen nation" and the belief that America is/was a "Christian nation."

My thesis is this: to "mind the gap" that I've been describing, the Christian tradition—especially evangelicals in America—have to take the post-secular challenge and re-examine their mythology. In MacIntyrian terms, the current cultural climate is forcing evangelicals to examine their beliefs and to account for the rising constituency of "Nones" that have left the church for greener spiritual pastures. And much like the geocentric universe of Galileo's day, the belief that America is a chosen nation or a Christian nation needs to be reframed to account for reality and to be more faithful to the Hebrew and Christian Scriptures.

It will be helpful here to give the skeletal definition of evangelical Christianity with which I am working. There are two marks of evangelicals: (1) evangelicals would describe having a personal relationship with God that started with some form of an Augustinian "conversion" experience—there was a time that they made faith in Christ their own and can usually give a general description of that time and decision. (2) Evangelicals take the Hebrew and Christian Scriptures as authoritative for life and faith. In the spirit of the Reformation, evangelicals take the "priesthood of all believers" as sacrosanct, so interpretive questions and disagreements about the proper understanding of the Scriptures are left to each individual, worshipping community, or formal ecclesiastical authority to decide. Because Christianity is a relatively old tradition, several sub-traditions have developed throughout its history. These are represented in catechisms and statements of faith that outline the boundaries of orthodox belief and praxis. There are several important historical sub-traditions, like Catholicism and Eastern Orthodoxy that predate Protestantism, but for my purposes in talking about the role and boundaries of religious practice in American democracy, Protestantism remains the focus. And within Protestantism, much more could be said about mainline Protestantism that is often associated with "liberal" or "progressive" Christianity, or Protestantism in non-white contexts—especially the role of the black church in America.

3. Hughes, *Myths America Lives By*.

But white Protestant evangelicals seem to get a lot of attention these days in the political conversation, so that is where my focus will lie.

Many evangelicals argue vehemently (and sometimes in a shrill tone) that Christians should have a central role in shaping public policy decisions because of America's deep "Christian heritage." The argument goes like this: The war on Christian orthodoxy that began in the late nineteenth century has knocked America off the path to the good life that the founders set it on; a return to those roots will help recover the virtue and prosperity that America once had (in the 2016 presidential election cycle this sentiment was captured in Donald Trump's slogan, "Make America great again"). Evangelicals sometimes go to great lengths to cultivate this mythology (see the controversy over David Barton's book on Thomas Jefferson, as an example)[4] and often long nostalgically for simpler times when you could pray in school, have the Ten Commandments in government buildings, and LGBTQ questions were tucked away neatly in the storage room of public consciousness.

This idea of America as a "chosen nation" and a "Christian nation" developed out of a borrowed metaphor from Ancient Judaism. It is the image of the patriarchs and monarchs—an ancestral heritage that confers special rights, obligations, and privileges to be the caretakers of culture. It is borrowed from the nascent stages of a theocracy that was established on the Mosaic covenant: if you follow God's laws the nation will be blessed, but if you are not faithful to God the nation will be cursed (Deut 28). The Puritans carried this image of the people of God finding a "new promised land," as their attempts at instigating spiritual renewal through national politics in England were continually frustrated, and they looked for more fertile ground for a covenantal nation in America. This image of America as a covenantal nation has both religious and secular meanings: For evangelicals, it means that America has a special role to play in the world and needs to be preserved to fulfill its role. The secular meaning spills into the idea of American exceptionalism in international politics. These meanings carry a great deal of weight in America's understanding of itself, so it is important to understand these borrowed images from Judaism.

In his book *In God's Shadow: Politics in the Hebrew Bible*, Michael Walzer argues that the Israelites had two senses of political obligation: (1) an inherited obligation to God through their ancestral connection to Abraham, Isaac, and Jacob; and (2) a voluntary obligation based on their

4. Schuessler, "Hard Truth for Author."

communal agreement to the Mosaic Covenant at Mount Sinai. As the political life of Israel developed around the covenant, blessings and curses were given as a consequence of their faithfulness. Early on in their national life, Israel had a decentralized form of government in tribal judges where God was their king. Later, they requested a king (in order to be like other nations) and the charismatic leader (the judge) was replaced by the magisterial leader. Israel's political life became centralized around the king and the king's family.[5] Walzer goes on to argue that the monarchy gave occasion for the rise of the office of prophet—an individual called by God to speak to the king, the nation, or the surrounding nations about their faithfulness to Yahweh. The government became the representative for the people—not a representative of the people—and thus the faithfulness of the king determined the fate of the nation. The monarchy's long history of unfaithfulness, despite prophetic warnings of judgment, resulted in Babylonian captivity and exile: the destruction of the temple, the sacking of Jerusalem, and the deportation of the aristocratic leadership.

The parallels drawn with American Christianity can be seen in references to 2 Chronicles 7:14 in denominational and ecumenical gatherings: "If my people, who are called by name, will humble themselves and seek my face and pray and turn from their wicked ways, then I will hear their voice and forgive their sin, and heal their land." Hughes argues that this notion of a chosen or covenantal nation was embedded in William Tyndale's English translation of the Bible that animated the Puritans during their struggle to renew England. Captured by what Calvin was doing in Geneva, Switzerland, the Puritans hoped that God would bless England if the government would take the laws of God seriously. When their reformation efforts were continually frustrated, they sought "more fertile soil" in the wilderness of America. The Puritans used Exodus imagery to stir the imagination for what God could do on new soil—this story often stirs the imagination of oppressed peoples and gives hope in revolutionary efforts.[6] For the Puritans, England was Egypt, the Atlantic Ocean was the Red Sea, and America was the new promised land. In setting sail for America on the *Arbella*, John Winthrop said these words in his address to the men aboard the ship: "Thus stands the case between God and us. We are entered into a Covenant with Him for this work . . . We shall find that the God of Israel is

---

5. Walzer, *In God's Shadow*, 60.

6. Walzer makes this argument in his book *Exodus and Revolution*.

among us . . . For we must consider that we shall be as a City upon a hill."[7] Both Benjamin Franklin and Thomas Jefferson (neither should be taken as evangelical by any means) suggested using imagery of the Exodus for the seal of the United States. Hughes traces the power that this metaphor carried through times of national crisis in America's history, and George Marsden emphasizes this narrative in his book *The Twilight of the American Enlightenment*.[8] Marsden suggests that the antithesis between America as a Christian, democratic, and capitalist nation and the former Soviet Union as an atheist, communist, and socialist nation reinvigorated and cemented the idea of national covenant at the twilight of liberal Christianity and the increase of evangelical influence in culture as World War II ended and the Cold War between the Soviet Union and America escalated.[9]

Evangelical movements that matured in the shadow of the Cold War were intent on keeping the "America as a Christian Nation" motif alive and flourishing. The idea of a "crusade" to recapture America's heritage of Christianity filled all sectors of society. Billy Graham's public lectures were known as the "Billy Graham Crusades," and during that time Campus Crusade for Christ was born (1951).[10] In Campus Crusade for Christ's story, the university was a small microcosm of what was happening in broader Western culture. What started as a place for Christian formation and pastoral training had transformed into a bastion for "liberal" and sometimes "anti-Christian" ideas. This drift from "Christian beginnings" to a secular and liberal ethos needed to be addressed and returned to its Christian heritage.[11]

On the heels of the cultural revolution of the 1960s, the Moral Majority was formed to stem the tide of "secularism" and "liberalism"—two "isms" that reflected the decline of Christian influence and signaled an impending immoral social trajectory. The Moral Majority was established to mobilize a majority that still held "Christian values" and to reassert those values in the halls of power. Much has been written about this move and its relative lack of success,[12] but it is clear that the driving force to look to the

7. Buck, *Religious Myths*, 29.

8. Marsden, *Twilight of the American Enlightenment*.

9. Ibid., 125.

10. Campus Crusade for Christ changed its name to Cru in 2011. See Campus Crusade for Christ, "Campus Crusade."

11. Marsden, *The Soul of the American University*.

12. For two examples of the failure of this political move, see Hunter, *To Change the*

political to undo this secular trajectory was formed around the notion that America is (was) a "Christian nation."

Where am I going with all of this? The shift from a covenant-centered, decentralized political life led by charismatic judges to a centralized monarchy in Jewish history has striking parallels to the shift from charismatic apostolic leadership and decentralized church organization to the centralization of the church with the Roman Empire under Constantine. With this shift, the fate of the church now rested with the success or failure of the Roman Empire. Membership within the church shifted from voluntary commitment to the Lordship of Christ (over/against the lordship of Caesar) to inherited membership (being born under Roman rule and authority), the first stages of Christendom in the West and, as I mentioned above, what Yoder calls the "Constantinian compromise." For Christians, the story of this shift is the background framework for the democratic revolutions in both England and America; and it is the driving metaphor for evangelical involvement in politics in the mid-twentieth century. The myths of America as a "chosen nation" and, consequently, America as a "Christian" nation are residue from the church's gradual move away from being a minority presence in the first two centuries of its existence to the ones who held the levers of power. And it is a move away from the model of servant-leadership to seeing oneself as cultural caretakers.

My contention is this: evangelicals in America borrow theocratic metaphors from Judaism without a Scriptural basis for a national calling, a national covenant, a hereditary mark of membership, a centralized place for worship, a territory marked out by God's providential care, or specific laws given to govern the cultic and political life of the followers of Christ. I want to argue that, to recover the authenticity of the Christian tradition and faithfulness to the teachings of Jesus in a post-secular and highly politicized age (a MacIntyrian reframing), evangelicals have to exchange theocratic and monarchial analogies between Israel and the church for a "return to exile."

Because the Christian church is under a "new covenant" (Heb 8:6–13), an international community (not tied to a distinct place), voluntary (and not inherited), without a political structure (it is political, but not a polity), and stripped of any sense of centralization (there is no central place of worship like a temple), the New Testament writers assume that the relationship

---

World; Thomas and Dobson, *Blinded by Might*. I will address this in fuller detail in chapter 5.

of the church to the Roman Empire will be like the relationship between the Israelites and Babylon. This assumption is apparent in the writings of 1 Peter and the Revelation of John when they both refer to Rome as "Babylon."

The author of 1 Peter addresses the letter to the "exiles of the dispersion in Pontus, Galatia, Cappadocia, Asia, and Bithnia"—exiles chosen by God. In chapter 2, he refers to his audience as a "chosen race, a royal priesthood, a holy nation, God's own people . . . Once you were not a people, but now you are God's people; once you had not received mercy, but now you have received mercy" (1 Pet 2:9–11). Here the author of 1 Peter uses two analogies to communicate to these churches: (1) a chosen people, and (2) exiles. The author is drawing from a Jewish heritage to communicate that the church formed around Jesus Christ is chosen. Where they were once separated and excluded from the chosen people by birth status, they are now voluntarily included through their faith in Christ. But like much of Jewish history, the church is also in an exilic state—a stranger, an alien—never quite at home in its host culture. The *diaspora* captures this twofold imagery. A chosen people scattered among but not absorbed into the nations.[13]

This does not provide a theological doctrine of supercession; rather, the author is reminding his readers that their experience with Rome is nothing that the people of God had not been through before. And despite the primarily Roman and Gentile context, the early followers of Jesus in these cities would be familiar with these stories. They would be familiar with the Jewish narrative in the Torah of their exilic existence in Egypt and the Lord's deliverance through Moses. They would be reminded of the exilic existence in Babylon and the partial, but not completely, fulfilled return. They were aware of the messianic eschatology that developed out of the hope of God's deliverance. And they would be told stories of Joseph, Daniel, Esther, and Jeremiah—heroes of ancient Judaism who flourished in exile.

The author of 1 Peter is a prominent example of this kind of theology, but other New Testament writers assume the ubiquity of the Roman Empire in their admonitions on how to live faithfully to Jesus Christ in a culture that might cut against Christian virtue. Hebrews 11:13 states this about the great heroes of the faith in the Hebrew Scriptures: "All of these died in faith without having received the promises, but from a distance they saw and greeted them. They confessed that they were strangers and exiles on the earth, for people who speak in this way make it clear that they are seeking

---

13. Levine and Brettler, *Jewish Annotated New Testament*, 437.

a homeland." And in the Gospel of John, Jesus is recorded praying for his disciples: "I am not asking you to take them out of the world . . . They do not belong to the world, just as I do not belong to the world . . . As you have sent me into the world, so I have sent them into the world" (John 17:15–18). It is difficult to think that the writers of the New Testament could imagine that within four centuries, Christianity would become the official religion of the Roman Empire; and that being faithful to Jesus Christ would mean protecting Roman culture.

Walter Pilgrim argues that the New Testament does not take a monolithic stand in articulating the church's relationship to the state, but "exhibits a range of responses from subordination to resistance that reflects the early church's theological and ethical evaluation of the state in varying historical circumstances."[14] For Pilgrim, three responses stand out in the New Testament: (1) subordination, (2) critical distancing, and (3) resistance toward a totalitarian and idolatrous state. Pilgrim maintains that faithfulness to Christ takes varied forms in different cultural contexts. Thus, a measure of discernment is necessary relative to the church's place in culture.

It is also important to note that the New Testament is relatively silent and ambiguous about secular government in general. In no place does it endorse a particular kind of government, such as democracy, and the two most prominent passages that talk about government are somewhat ambiguous about its role. Romans 13:1–7 states,

> Let every person be subject to the governing authorities; for there is no authority except from God, and those authorities that exist have been instituted by God. Therefore whoever resists authority resists what God has appointed, and those who resist will incur judgment. For rulers are not a terror to good conduct, but to bad. Do you wish to have no fear of the authority? Then do what is good, and you will receive its approval; for it is God's servant for your good. But if you do what is wrong, you should be afraid, for the authority does not bear the sword in vain! It is the servant of God to execute wrath on the wrongdoer. Therefore one must be subject, not only because of wrath but also because of conscience. For the same reason you also pay taxes, for the authorities are God's servants, busy with this very thing. Pay to all what is due them—taxes to whom taxes are due, revenue to whom revenue is due, respect to whom respect is due, honor to whom honor is due.

1 Peter 2:13–17 echoes these same themes:

14. Pilgrim, *Uneasy Neighbors*, 2.

> For the Lord's sake accept the authority of every human institution, whether of the emperor as supreme, or of governors, as sent by him to punish those who do wrong and to praise those who do right. For it is God's will that by doing right you should silence the ignorance of the foolish. As servants of God, live as free people, yet do not use your freedom as a pretext for evil. Honor everyone. Love the family of believers. Fear God. Honor the emperor.

These are the two most prominent passages that talk about secular governments, and neither give criteria that positions of leadership require a person to be a follower of Christ. They speak of two roles for any government and institution of authority—reward good and punish evil; both words, "good" and "evil," here leave a lot of room for interpretation of what they mean.

To put what I've argued for so far in terms of a tradition: to be faithful to Jesus in its public life—to mind the gap—the first step that the church must take is toward its first-century Jewish roots. This will mean abandoning the misguided mythology of America as a chosen nation and as a Christian nation and embracing a "return to exile." These were false beliefs that needed to be challenged and reframed to more accurately reflect how the New Testament talks about the relationship between the church and the world.

Some prominent evangelical writers have been arguing recently that the state of the church in America is in exile. Russell Moore's book, *Onward*, is an example of this trend.[15] Moore is the president of the Southern Baptist Convention's Ethics and Religious Liberty Commission (ERLC). In 2008 he guest-hosted the Albert Mohler radio program and interviewed Mark Dever and Stanley Hauerwas on patriotism in the pews of our churches.[16] In this interview, he clearly articulates a view of Christian patriotism. Without any distinctions, Christians are supposed to be thankful for the freedoms we have in this country, especially religious freedoms. In *Onward*, Moore argues that the church is now a prophetic minority instead of a moral majority. He laments the theological and political gymnastics it took to bring a nominally friendly political candidate into the range of appreciation and affirmation by the evangelical community. The most recent example of this is the 2016 presidential campaign and election: 80 percent of white evangelicals voted for Donald Trump.[17] In the run-up to the election, several

15. Moore, *Onward*.

16. Mohler, "Should We Be Patriots?"

17. Smith and Martínez, "How the Faithful Voted."

articles by evangelical leaders surfaced in support of Trump. For example, see Wayne Grudem's "Why Voting for Trump Is a Morally Good Choice,"[18] and popular evangelical author Eric Metaxas's rhetorical question in his op-ed in the *Wall Street Journal*, "Should Christians Vote for Trump?", in which the answer is clearly yes.[19] Metaxas's argument is that the alternative (Hillary Clinton) is so bad that Donald Trump is the best candidate to vote for so that Christians can advance their political platform.

Moore argues for the church's return to a prophetic minority in order to recover the authenticity of the gospel. Other evangelicals have been captured by the prophetic encouragement of Jeremiah to Israel during Babylonian captivity in Jeremiah 29:4–7:

> Thus says the Lord of hosts, the God of Israel, to all the exiles whom I have sent into exile from Jerusalem to Babylon: Build houses and live in them; plant gardens and eat what they produce. Take wives and have sons and daughters; take wives for your sons, and give your daughters in marriage, that they may bear sons and daughters; multiply there, and do not decrease. But seek the welfare of the city where I have sent you into exile, and pray to the Lord on its behalf, for in its welfare you will find your welfare.[20]

This more frequent use of exilic imagery is a clear case of MacIntyre's notion of an external epistemological crisis forcing evangelical Christians to re-examine their beliefs. The precipitous drop in cultural influence and losses in statewide and national legislative initiatives is causing a reconsideration of deeply held beliefs. This reconsideration is not motivated by theological reflection, but by cultural marginalization. It is the loss of the belief that Christians (especially evangelicals) should hold a special place at the table of public discourse because of America's godly heritage; and the belief that evangelical political hegemony (read moral majority) was the antidote to sweeping cultural changes. More than false, these two beliefs obscure the authenticity of the Christian message and nudge Christianity to the margins of political discourse. And this lack of cultural status is reframing the context of Christian faith in America.

To recover an authentic understanding of the church's relationship to culture, N. T. Wright has argued that we must understand the New

18. Grudem, "Why Voting for Trump Is a Morally Good Choice."
19. Metaxas, "Should Christians Vote for Trump?"
20. Keller, "Serving the City."

Testament in its Second Temple Jewish context.[21] The writers of the Scriptures are trying to make sense out of their Jewish expectations of a promised messianic restoration and renewal in light of the "Jesus events." His contention is that Second Temple Judaism was never quite free from exile despite a proximate location in Ancient Israel and the presence of a reconstructed temple; they were still operating in the shadows of the ubiquity of the Roman Empire and therefore were aliens in their own land. This creates a discontent in the Jewish community that results in the successive attempts at revolution (66 CE and 132 CE respectively). This is the framework that the New Testament writers inherit as they write to the nascent groups of people who are following Jesus—the early church. Thus, it is quite easy to see how these writers would talk about their context as exilic.

This "return to exile" (a different posture for the church in America and the Western world) is fraught with problems and possibilities. It is difficult to anticipate all of the problems, but here are at least three: First, it will be a difficult transition filled with accusations of heresy, public denouncements, and fear-mongering about the decline of America. Nobody goes into exile voluntarily. This is an internal problem as the Evangelical Church re-negotiates its relationship with culture. People who imagine themselves in power, or who have created an expectation that they should have influence, rarely volunteer to give up their perceived power—especially if they see themselves as benevolent or having some corner on "truth." There are parallels to this problem in the pages of the Gospels. There were at least four responses to living in the shade of Rome: (1) accommodation to the culture (Sadducees), (2) maintaining the purity of the Jewish tradition (Pharisees), (3) withdrawal from culture altogether (Essenes), and (4) revolution (Zealots). These are broad generalizations, but seemingly reflective of the types of responses that can come when living as aliens in a foreign and sometimes hostile land. And each of these groups thought that the others were wrong in some way.

I also want to draw some parallels from the first-century responses to Rome to H. Richard Niebuhr's classic work on the relationship between the church and culture, *Christ and Culture*.[22] In his book, Niebuhr outlines five responses that the church has had with culture: (1) Christ against culture (Anabaptists), (2) Christ above culture (Catholics), (3) Christ and culture in paradox (Lutherans), (4) Christ in culture (Mainline Protestants), and

21. Wright, *Jesus and the Victory of God*, 91.
22. Niebuhr, *Christ and Culture*.

(5) Christ the Transformer of culture (Calvinists). Anyone who has read Niebuhr's book carefully recognizes that he skewed his articulation of each of these perspectives to demonstrate the veracity of "Christ the Transformer of culture." In both first-century Jewish responses to Rome and contemporary alternatives of the church's response to Western culture, there was and will be accusations of getting it wrong, of being unfaithful to Christ. In Essay II of *To Change the World*, Hunter takes at least three different Christian traditions to task on how they viewed the church's role in culture.[23]

The counter-example to this problem is Jesus. The gospels record a tension between Jesus and each of the four groups described above in his ministry. Jesus would not accommodate himself to the Roman government, nor did he advocate for withdrawal. As we saw earlier, he prayed that his disciples would not be "of the world," but he kept them "in the world" (John 17:6–19). Jesus did not affirm the revolutionaries, but commanded his followers to "love their enemies" (Matt 5:18–48). And he consistently blew open the boundaries of what pure tradition meant in his day (Luke 11:37–54). Niebuhr's first four categories parallel these same reactions, and he argues that they are inadequate responses by the church toward culture. Maybe this is why he added a fifth category, "Christ the Transformer of culture"—Jesus never affirmed the adequacy of any one posture found in the Jewish community's response to Rome. But he also never affirmed Rome as the ultimate answer (Matt 22:15–22). Walter Wink calls this "Jesus' third way."

The second problem related to the transition to exile is that it will include misunderstanding, harassment, and possibly persecution or suffering. This is an external problem, as the culture tries to negotiate its relationship to the church. Exiles (and minority groups in general) are looked upon suspiciously, and are the first to be accused of undermining the "stability" of the culture. This was the accusation against Christians that the author of 1 Peter was addressing—Christian liberty and egality were destabilizing the *huastafeln* of Roman society. In contemporary settings, politicians prey on the fear of decline and instability of the nation during election cycles—the villains in this story end up to be those that do not hold the religious beliefs of majority culture or are not like majority culture in appearance and practice. The 2016 presidential race focused on the problems of America and how "outsiders" have contributed to those problems. What is wrong with America is the "radical Islamists" and illegal immigrants—those that

23. Hunter, *To Change the World*, 99–193.

are not like "us" in custom or habit. A corollary to the idea that exiles are always misunderstood and may suffer is that sometimes they can suffer for the wrong things. It is quite easy to interpret a challenge to a political position or a law against discrimination as "suffering" for the sake of Christ. A recent example of this kind of perceived suffering is when a Colorado bakery refused to make a cake for a same-sex couple because it violated their conscience and definition of marriage. Their case received quite a lot of attention, and ultimately the Colorado courts ruled against their reasons for refusing to make the cake.[24] The difficulty here is in discernment. What are the things that are worth standing up for despite the consequences and what are the things that are just cultural attachments to the good news of the gospel of Christ? At best, as followers of Jesus, Christians will never be at home in any culture—they will always be cultural outsiders. And at worst, Christians will suffer violence as a consequence of faithfulness to Christ, as many currently do throughout the world.

The third problem is that a return to exile also means giving up the last word in culture. The last word is the definitive word, the political word, the legislative word, and the coercive word. It comes with the authority of the state to pass and enforce laws. The last word is also a comfortable word. It is comfortable, because if you have it, you get your way—your good is defined for everyone else and enforced. Any group—Democrats, Republicans, Independents, religious groups, or any secondary associations in society—think that their way is the best possible way to get to the good. But it can also be comfortable for the opposite reason: if a good is rejected, you are excused from social responsibility. It is easy to wash one's hands of social responsibility if the crowd goes in a different direction.

Again, the writers of the gospels hold up the model of Christ to counteract this tendency to always get in the last word. During the passion narratives of the gospels, it is always the world that has the last word. The religious leaders have the last word, "blasphemy"; the crowd has the last word in Jesus' public trial, "crucify him" and "we want Barabbas"; Pilate has the last word (though he tries to absolve himself from responsibility) in the verdict. The Roman guards have the last word by mocking him, "Hail, King of the Jews," beating him, and spitting on him; and the criminals who were crucified alongside of him even had a last word—"the bandits who were crucified with him also taunted him in the same way." But Jesus' last words are words to God, not to the worldly powers; and they are curious words,

24. Smith and Martínez, "How the Faithful Voted."

really: "My God, my God, why have you forsaken me?" and "Father, forgive them; for they do not know what they are doing" (Matt 27:46; Luke 23:34 respectively).

The story does not end with the Passion narrative; there is an account of a resurrection, and this fits into a consistent thread of narratives throughout Jewish history: Moses and Pharaoh, Joseph and his brothers, Joshua and Jericho, Gideon and Midian, Daniel and Nebuchadnezzar, and Esther and Xerxes. Faithfulness to Yahweh means allowing God to have the last word. Again, Michael Walzer has some insightful comments on the tension "God's people" feel when trying to accomplish God's purposes. He states,

> A God engaged in history is a dangerous God, for it is always possible to read his intentions and try to help him out, usually by killing his enemies. In principle, God doesn't need help—the prophets are absolutely clear about this—but in practice, more often than not, his enemies seem to have the upper hand, or he moves with such slowness that we fear never to see their final defeat.[25]

For Christians, God has the last word because only God has the proper perspective on the world. Within the Christian tradition, two doctrines should promote a kind of Christian humility that might give space for God to have the last word: the doctrine of human finiteness (we are limited in our knowledge) and the doctrine of human depravity (that we tend to bend reason and morality in our own direction). There is more to these doctrines than this simple caricature, but this simplicity should give the Christian tradition pause in always having to assert the last word in culture.

Further, Walzer argues that we have flipped the script on the importance of Christian involvement in the political. In his book, *Revolution of the Saints*, he concludes with a prophetic word for Christians in our time: "the last word always belongs to the worldlings and not to the saints. It is a complacent word and it comes when salvation in all its meanings is no longer a problem. But the saints have what is more interesting; the first word. *They set the stage of history for the new order.*"[26] The last word is a complacent and comfortable word—it is a word for those who are not in exile, but have some control over the way things will go. Faithfulness to Jesus, however, means that Christians might have the more interesting word, the creative word. Here I want to pause for a moment and ask the

25. Walzer, *In God's Shadow*, 206.

26. Walzer, *Revolution of the Saints*, 319. Emphasis mine.

question, "Which best describes evangelicals in America: last-word people or creative first-word people?" The saints were supposed to be out in front in culture, connected to people and the needs of the community, and taking concrete action to help demonstrate the love and wisdom of God.

This is a natural transition to begin to outline the possibilities of exile. As above, I will highlight three. I will say more about the potential for Christians as they recover the first-word impulse that Walzer is describing here in chapter 6, for now here are some beneficial consequences to being a voluntary minority voice in culture. First, there is the possibility of a deeper faithfulness to Christ. According to 1 Peter 1:6–8: "In this you rejoice, even if now for a little while you have had to suffer various trials, so that the genuineness of your faith—being more precious than gold that, though perishable, is tested by fire—may be found to result in praise and glory and honor when Jesus Christ is revealed." Being out of sync with culture produces a kind of tension that strips away the cultural parasites that attach themselves to the gospel. Examples of these kinds of parasites are: you have to be a Republican to be a Christian; you have to be a Calvinist to be a Christian; you have to be a capitalist to be Christian; i.e., you cannot be a (fill in the blank), you have to believe (fill in the blank) to be a Christian. When the church accommodates itself to culture, litmus tests are necessary to define the "serious" Christians from the "nominal" Christians—the "radical" from the "complacent." This was true in the fourth century and continues to be true today. Tension should be welcome as the Christian tradition works toward following Christ more faithfully.

While tension seems to produce a more pure faith, like refining the dross from gold, the pressure of exile can also produce excellence—like turning coal into a diamond. The Jewish roots of Christianity illustrate this point clearly. The stories of Joseph, Moses, Daniel, and Esther are stories of God using the excellence, the education, the outward characteristics, and the wisdom of these men and women to benefit God's people and bless the world. More will be said about this later as I draw out the characteristics that these exilic figures share in common. These stories are embedded in Jewish history as a way of encouraging those who follow Yahweh to stay faithful in the midst of difficulty. Survival in exile requires a kind of standing out in culture. Hunter argues that it is the "elites," who exist and do their work at the margins of a culture, that are actually the ones who are the catalysts for change (those who have demonstrated excellence in their vocation or have a particular social standing, but aren't at the centers of the levers of power and influence).[27] Jeffrey Stout shares a similar conclusion in his book, *Blessed are the Organized*.[28] Stout argues that grassroots organization requires sponsorship by an elite class to actually make change.

The historical challenge that Hunter raises is that evangelicals are somewhat inept at cultivating cultural elites. This is also what Mark Noll argued in *The Scandal of the Evangelical Mind*.[29] Evangelicals have a difficult time cultivating elites because of the fear of accommodation (which is somewhat ironic given their comfort with worldly politics and war) or heterodoxy—that a field of research might take one outside of accepted orthodoxy. This kind of cultural excellence puts a strain on faith because it places one at the intersection of different traditions. I contend that this intersection actually creates a stronger faith for those who are willing to embrace the tensions; but produces a weaker faith for those who shrink from these kinds of challenges. Will being in exile nudge Christianity to recover its creative impulse, or will it push Christianity into the backwaters of nostalgia—longing for a return to a bygone era?

There is a subtle temptation in this possibility of cultivating excellence—the temptation to cultivate elites to regain power. In the Christian tradition, cultivating excellence in individuals is intrinsically good; it is anchored in the doctrine of creation—that God has given gifts to all persons and those gifts are supposed to contribute to the flourishing (Hebrew word *shalom*) of all people. It is also anchored in the doctrine of common grace: that all of humanity shares in the goodness of God's creation and that truth, wisdom, and goodness are available to all people (Phil 4:1–8). Excellence, captivated by the redemption of Christ, is meant to encourage the flourishing of human beings that are made in God's image and live in God's world, but that have been scarred and corrupted by sin.

So far, the possibilities of exile include a deeper faithfulness to Christ and the possibility for the cultivation of excellence. Finally, there is the possibility of compassion and creativity. I've just smuggled two possibilities in one; but I think that they go together. Empathy comes with experience, and we develop a deeper compassion when we enter into the situation of the other and truly understand their experience. The Christian tradition has a

27. Hunter, *To Change the World*.
28. Stout, *Blessed Are the Organized*.
29. Noll, *Scandal of the Evangelical Mind*.

history of paying attention to people on the margins. Catholics call this the "preferential treatment of the poor." The widow, the captive, the orphan, and the poor are categories of people on the margins of society that the Hebrew and Christian Scriptures put at the center of God's concern. But sometimes, when you hold the levers of power and influence in society, focus shifts to other places—namely, preserving power and focusing on governmental and institutional help.

3

Democracy Needs a Complement

IN CHAPTER 1, I argued that the democratic tradition is the best way to organize a pluralistic society. At its best, democracy allows the variegated voices of many different communities a seat at the proverbial table of public policy questions. In Michael Walzer's terms, democracy is the best way to organize a society around a plurality of goods.[1] In theory, democracy as a tradition has a minimalist ethic that allows for the greatest of freedoms for the most people. But inherent in its strengths, the democratic tradition has several weaknesses. In this chapter, I will highlight four of those weaknesses and argue that the democratic tradition needs a complementary tradition to carry it forward.

First, the democratic tradition will always and necessarily marginalize some citizens—utilitarian calculations of the good leaves some goods unrealized. The greatest good for the greatest number means that there will be some who will not be represented with the goods that the majority legislates. Further, when some goods are legislated, the just distribution of those goods may not satisfy every citizen's perceived wants or needs. At best, this leaves some communities dissatisfied, and at worst, it marginalizes and oppresses them. Second, it is difficult to make positive claims about the direction of "society" without common moral assumptions and language. One person's progress is another's "moral decline." This can be seen in conflicting views of the cultural revolution of the 1960s. For some, they finally found a voice (minorities, women, the LGBTQ community); for others, those gains are counterbalanced or overwhelmed by the loss of

---

1. Walzer, *Spheres of Justice*, 303.

a certain kind of sexual ethic, the loss of a spiritual presence in the public conversation, and a blatant disregard for God and the Bible. Third, in its practice of giving and receiving reasons in the public conversation over goods and how they are distributed, the democratic tradition creates conversation and conflict, but does not have a mechanism to resolve that conflict, except by the assertion of power through legislation. This is closely related to the second weakness and is creating an ethos of the strong over the weak, the educated over the uneducated, or the wealthy over the poor. This creates resentment for those who see no hope in having their voice heard. And finally, fourth, the democratic tradition can create a tyranny of the majority—where the majority is morally wrong (either intentionally or unwittingly), but has the power. These weaknesses have different iterations as democracy takes different forms, but let us look at an example of each in our own American context.

It does not take much searching to find places where those in the minority got pushed to the margins in a democracy. America has a sordid past with this particular weakness, and it continues today. Thomas Jefferson famously wrote these words in the Declaration of Independence, "We hold these truths to be self-evident, that all men are created equal, that they are endowed by their Creator with certain unalienable Rights, that among these are Life, Liberty and the pursuit of Happiness" while at the same time owning slaves.[2] It is also important to note the male-centric language in the Declaration of Independence and that women were not granted the right to vote until 1920. While we do not have time to elaborate on the particulars of these examples, we can acknowledge that marginalization in the history of democracy is prevalent. The Three-Fifths Compromise was ironically argued for by Southern slave owners to increase their representation in the government, while the Northerners did not want to count any slaves as citizens.[3] As late as 1857, the Dred Scott decision by the Supreme Court declared that slaves did not have the rights of citizens and that congress could not prohibit slavery.[4] After the North's victory in the Civil War, blacks in America were granted their freedom, but suffered under Jim Crow laws

2. "Declaration of Independence," https://www.archives.gov/founding-docs/declaration-transcript.

3. "What Was the Three Fifths Compromise?" http://constitution.laws.com/three-fifths-compromise.

4. "Dred Scott v. Sandford: Primary Documents of American History (Virtual Programs & Services, Library of Congress)," https://www.loc.gov/rr/program/bib/ourdocs/DredScott.html.

in the South that kept blacks "separate but equal" until the *Brown v. Board of Education* case ended the segregation of public education. In his famous "I Have a Dream" speech, Martin Luther King Jr. argued that America had not fulfilled its promises that it made as far back as the Declaration of Independence. And Michelle Alexander, in her book *The New Jim Crow: Mass Incarceration in the Age of Colorblindness,* argues that the prison-industrial complex and the American judicial system continue to marginalize and oppress a disproportionate number of young black and brown men.[5] This is a 250-year arc of marginalization for black men and women in America— there has been some progress, but more needs to be made. This is just a cursory overview of an injustice of some at the hands of the majority in a democracy. There is not enough space to attend to the other ethnic, cultural, sexual, religious, and economic minorities that fall outside the range of goods that those in power work toward legislating.

Second, finding common moral language to adjudicate between different goods in society and how those goods will impact future generations in a pluralistic public square is difficult, if not impossible. This is the postmodern problem that I alluded to in the introduction. We recognize that each large-scale tradition has its own beliefs, texts, and authorities that shape its way of reasoning and moral formation. But smaller communities do as well. I am from a small town in Western Montana; in college I met and dated a woman from the South. We shared many things, including our common Christian commitments, but I made one big mistake when I met her parents for the first time: I called them by their first names. In my moral world, it is quite natural to call someone who you take to be a friend, or a potential friend by his or her first name—it's a sign of relationship. But in the South, to call someone you have met for the first time, especially someone older than you and a respected member of the community, by their first names was a sign of disrespect. They were very generous and gracious to me, but it was clear that I violated a moral norm of Southern culture. This is just a small example of a cultural clash, but an illustration of the prior commitments that each of us brings to moral conversations that create misunderstandings and moral conflict—and these kinds of conversations only get more difficult as larger and more established traditions cross moral paths. In conversations about moral issues, these kinds of conclusions are called "particular or immediate judgments." They are our immediate responses to a moral situation in judging an action right or wrong. These judgments are

5. Alexander, *The New Jim Crow.*

usually anchored in the family and culture we grew up in so they are made without deliberation. The more pluralistic a community becomes, the less agreements and assumptions are shared. This makes moral conversations difficult.

Glen Stassen has argued that there are at least sixteen factors or "dimensions" to moral decision-making. Without articulating all sixteen, the essence of Stassen's argument is that any one of the sixteen could be different in a conversation about moral goods, and how those goods should be distributed. These differences can be subtle, but irreconcilable—especially if they are assumed and go unnoticed. Our assumptions about human nature, for example will shape how we view other people. I tried to show how a view of human nature shaped the evolution of the democratic tradition in chapter 1. The early religious influence on democracy motivated the idea of checks and balances—people are inherently "sinful" and will use power for their own purposes, so there must be a check put in place so that they cannot abuse their power. In contrast, Locke argued for the idea of the inherent goodness of humanity and a hoped-for social cooperation that would carry democracy forward. Stassen maintains that if we can understand and then identify which dimension is in conflict, we can isolate it and focus on resolving the conflict. Another practical example is how we address poverty in America. We may agree that it is a threat to the future of our society; but we disagree on how to address the problem—how to define a strategy for social change. One way to address the problem may be to work through economic stimulus and the creation of new jobs, but another may be to provide the poor with a social safety net like welfare. Stassen argues that the conversations get more difficult the deeper you go in a person's basic convictions (or worldview). Our more peripheral moral reasoning flows out of answers to the deeper questions of whether there is a God, what that God might be like, whether poverty is a result of choice or social circumstance, and what are the unalienable rights that are non-negotiable for every person in society. When we get to our basic convictions and conflict results, we usually end in colloquialisms or pithy aphorisms like, "well, that's true for you, but not for me," or "we will just have to agree to disagree."[6]

I have mentioned that one of the campaign slogans for President Donald Trump was "Make America Great Again." This aphorism is meant to inspire, but what gets left unanswered is: "Great for whom?" There is an assumption in this campaign slogan that America is in decline—that once

6. Stassen and Gushee, *Kingdom Ethics*.

there was a time when we were "great," but that time is in the past. This kind of nostalgia is a common refrain in many evangelical circles. The Christian right (the majority of them made up of evangelical Christians) laments the moral decline of America because it coincided with the removal of prayer in school, the removal of public postings of the Ten Commandments, the removal of Creche-specific exhibits on public property, the new possibility of no-fault divorce laws, birth control, and the Supreme Court's decision on *Roe v. Wade*. These were all lumped together and used to signal a loss of Judeo-Christian influence in American public life.

Robert P. Jones cites a Public Religion Research Institute (PRRI) survey that captured this difference in perspective. They asked the question, "Since the 1950s, do you think American culture and way of life has mostly changed for the better, or has it mostly changed for the worse?" 63 percent of the religiously unaffiliated answered that it had mostly changed for the better, while only 27 percent of white evangelicals answered affirmatively. Jones concluded that, "Overall, the pattern is unambiguous: most white Christians—along with groups in which they constitute a majority, like the Tea Party—believe that America is on a downhill slide, while strong majorities of most other groups in the country say things are improving."[7]

This narrative of moral decline and the misplaced theological analogy of America as the new "promised land" (see chapter 2) animated a shift in posture of many on the religious right. The emphasis rested on regaining the cultural influence that evangelicals once had through a new kind of involvement in politics. If the right people could be elected and the right judges appointed, then the moral decline of America could be rolled back into moral respectability and God may once again bless America with "prosperity." The religious right mobilized their infrastructure for an all-out political battle to reclaim a national Christian heritage. And thus in James Hunter's words, the "Culture Wars" began.[8]

The culture wars are just one small example of the difficulty to adjudicate between competing claims about the good. One person's progress is another's moral decline. Here, weaknesses two and three, as I have tried to articulate them above, are very closely related. Democracies create conversation and conflict. Everyone is welcome at the table of public discourse, either individually or representatively; but because we find it difficult to settle our competing moral claims, we resort to power—and political power

---

7. Jones, *End of White Christian America*, 85–87.

8. See Hunter, *Culture Wars*.

specifically. In the early stages of the formation of democracy in America, there was an assumed moral language that was shaped by a kind of Protestant civil religion (this idea of civil religion is what Scotty is arguing for in the foreword—without the exclusivity of Protestantism). The sharper edges of particularist Christian language were smoothed out to accommodate different Christian expressions, Enlightenment sensibilities about social cooperation, and other religious traditions altogether; this produced a kind of civil religion that functioned as a basis for moral conversation. To return to Thomas Jefferson's words in the Declaration of Independence, the "self-evident truths" that all men were created equal and "endowed by their Creator with certain unalienable Rights,"[9] reflects the language of this civil religion and the manner in which it framed the moral conversation—a combination of providential deism and Scottish Common Sense Realism. Alexis de Tocqueville reflected this sentiment in *Democracy in America*: "America is . . . the place in the world where the Christian religion has most preserved genuine powers over souls; and . . . the country in which [the Christian religion] exercises the greatest empire is at the same time the most enlightened and most free."[10]

Mark Noll has argued that Christian particularity, especially the use of the Bible in public discourse, was moved to the margins in the public square in the aftermath of the Civil War. In his book *The Civil War as a Theological Crisis*, Noll documents how each side of the war justified their participation and argued for their cause using biblical references. For the North, the broad Scriptural principles of equality, love, and justice stirred the religious sensibilities of the abolitionist movement. For the South, simple texts that acknowledged the presence of slavery and how slaves were to interact with their masters in both the Hebrew and the Christian Scriptures justified slavery. Noll maintains that this argument over the interpretation of the Scriptures was ultimately settled on the battlefield: "But the Civil War was won and slavery was abolished not by theological orthodoxy but by military might."[11] Noll's conclusion was that the Civil War "took the steam out of Protestant's moral energy" and set a course to remove Scripture from

---

9. "Declaration of Independence," https://www.archives.gov/founding-docs/declaration-transcript.

10. Tocqueville, *Democracy in America*, 278; quoted in Noll, *Civil War as a Theological Crisis*, 28.

11. Ibid., 160.

any justification of national public policy. This set the stage for a move toward secularizing the public square.

This secularizing trajectory has seemed to run its course. If a civil Protestant religion shaped the early formation of democracy in America, after the Civil War, the move toward secularism began to take its place. This caught full steam through the cultural revolution of the 1960s, as the amalgamation of historical circumstances cemented the notion that religion tends to do more harm than good. The dominant ethos of moral argument developed into a scorning of even civil religion in favor of appeals to rational, scientific, and humanitarian principles in secular language for public matters. Richard Rorty would argue in his early work that all appeals to religious language in public discourse are "conversation stoppers" and therefore should only be held privately (and eventually not held at all). If an argument cannot be made in "neutral" secular language, it should not be brought out in public. In his later work, Rorty would acknowledge that appeals to legislative goods in secular language are not always neutral and can be "conversation stoppers" as well.[12] An authoritative appeal to John Stuart Mill or Jeremy Bentham is similar to a fundamentalist appeal to the Bible. This recognition—that there are secular conversation stoppers, is a nod to the reality that there really is no neutral moral language and a signal that a strictly secular public square necessarily prejudices some out of the public conversation.

Finally, an inherent weakness in democracies is the problem of the tyranny of the majority. This is closely related to the first weakness, but builds on a consensus of public opinion to become oppressive—not only are people marginalized and excluded from certain goods, but with some historical reflection we come to realize that the majority was wrong altogether. A clear example of this weakness was the eugenics movement in the early twentieth-century in America and the sterilization laws that were put in place to "strengthen society."

The eugenics movement in America is often overshadowed by the atrocities of the Holocaust, but it can be argued that this movement developed earlier and had some influence on the Nazi idea of a "master race."[13] From the early sterilization laws in Indiana (1907) to the miscegenation laws that were overturned by the Supreme Court in *Loving v. Virginia*, various attempts at improving "human stock" through selective or surgical

12. Rorty, "Religion in the Public Square," 143.
13. Black, *War Against the Weak*.

sterilization were "performed for the public benefit . . . to maintain control within state institutions and to limit welfare costs."[14] This idea of perfecting humanity and improving society through selective breeding, forced sterilizations, and institutionalizing the weak had untold negative effects on many people in America and around the world. In 1937 one Gallup poll recorded that 45 percent of Americans supported euthanasia and in another poll, approximately 50 percent of the people surveyed affirmed the benefit of involuntary euthanasia for "hopeless invalids."[15] In 1927, Supreme Court Justice Oliver Wendell Holmes made this statement in the majority opinion on *Buck v. Bell*:

> It would be strange if it could not call upon those who already sap the strength of the State for these lesser sacrifices, often not felt to be such by those concerned, in order to prevent our being swamped with incompetence. It is better for all the world if, instead of waiting to execute degenerate offspring for crime or to let them starve for their imbecility, society can prevent those who are manifestly unfit from continuing their kind.[16]

These kinds of rulings, and the widespread popular opinion about the benefits of different eugenic strategies should cause us to pause and consider the tyrannical power of the majority. Again Walzer has some keen insights about this tyranny: "Political power protects us from tyranny . . . and itself becomes tyrannical. And it is for both these reasons that power is so much desired and so endlessly fought over."[17] Much is said about limited government and the three branches that balance political power, but as the examples above illustrate, there are moments in time when popular opinion and the legislative, judicial, and executive branches of government all swim in the wrong moral direction. Something more might be needed from citizens who, in Rorty's words, have commitments "elsewhere" (outside of social consensus).

It is precisely in these weaknesses that religion can complement the democratic tradition. Religious traditions are ideological, absolutist, and exclusive in the best sense—they tell a story about the good, the true, and the beautiful and how to get there. As I stated in chapter 1, this is why Richard Rorty has argued that religious persons make for less than ideal

14. Lombardo, *Century of Eugenics*.
15. Keith and Keith, *Intellectual Disability*.
16. "Buck v. Bell," https://www.law.cornell.edu/supremecourt/text/274/200.
17. Walzer, *Spheres of Justice*, 281.

citizens because they have commitments elsewhere: "non-theists make better citizens of democratic societies than theists."[18] They are "so heavenly minded that they are no earthly good," to use a popular cliché, or they are always the proverbial stick jammed into the spokes of the wheel of social progress. But these commitments "elsewhere" can be a hedge against the vulnerabilities that democracy creates. Religious commitments can bring the marginalized into focus as they respond to a subset of society that is suffering or struggling to be heard. They can set up structures and programs apart from the government to help meet needs or help take care of neglected or oppressed citizens. This is demonstrated in the multifarious faith-based nonprofit organizations that exist throughout civil society. Jeffrey Stout chronicles the impact of these types of religious groups in his book *Blessed Are the Organized*. Stout argues that synagogues, mosques, and churches play a unique role in helping to bring together the marginalized to have a greater voice in society.[19]

Paul Lombardo argues that it was after the Reformation when Queen Elizabeth I "secularized public philanthropy" by authorizing Poor Laws.[20] Before the Reformation, the church had been the primary caretaker of the poor, but after the Poor Laws were established, the responsibility shifted to the state. Lombardo continues, "By the time of the Industrial Revolution some 250 years later, both the numbers of the poor and the taxes to care for them had increased dramatically."[21] Lombardo is making this argument to demonstrate that once addressing the needs of the poor in society shifted to the state, citizens began to look at the poor as a burden. The people who were in poverty were the problem and needed to be addressed instead of viewing poverty as a systemic issue. This example is a reminder of the role that the church has played and continues to play in buoying those that do not benefit from "upward mobility."

Further, it is precisely because of its ideology and absolutism that the religious can speak out against an unjust action or structure of a governmental institution. This is an important "prophetic" role that the religious have often played in society. They have a moral framework anchored in something external—outside of "social consensus" and therefore can speak to its moral trajectory. We praise the prescient voices of luminary figures

18. Springs et al., "Pragmatism and Democracy."

19. Stout, *Blessed Are the Organized*.

20. Lombardo, *Century of Eugenics*, 169.

21. Ibid., 169.

like Dietrich Bonhoeffer in Germany, André Trocmé in France, William Wilberforce in England, and Dorothy Day and Martin Luther King Jr. in America; all of them spoke and acted against injustice with religious language and imagery. It is also in their commitments to something outside of themselves and apart from the social conventions of the day that religious citizens can maintain their moral fortitude over long periods of time. If something is right according to their sacred texts or beliefs, then social convention or the popularity of their position matters little to them in their efforts to do good. William Wilberforce demonstrated this kind of grit and resilience in his efforts to abolish slavery in England. He first introduced a bill to ban slavery into British Parliament in 1789; slavery was finally abolished in England in 1833. It took forty-four years of continued work that most often ran against the popular opinion of the powerful in English society to see his vision accomplished.[22]

In these two areas, the participation of religious citizens strengthens the democratic tradition in its natural weaknesses by providing a moral voice against the drift of the majority that develops in any form of democracy. Consequently, it is a benefit to invite the religious into the public square—with all of their religious language, religious motivations and religious reasons—even if we do not always agree with a particular religious community's vision of the good life. The contribution, creativity, and compassion of religious people can complement the structures of government. This was the notion of civil society and needs to be recovered for the religious. Religious individuals and/or religious institutions can help to initiate alternative programs or supplement those governmental programs that seek to address some of our more pressing social problems. As I mentioned in the introduction, still approximately 60 percent of Americans believe that religion can be a positive contribution in society—especially as it pays attention to the needs of the people who are most often found on the margins.

This is evident in the many examples of initiatives started by religious persons that are working to contribute to the good of society by addressing a particular need. In the San Francisco Bay Area, a faith-based nonprofit has worked to refurbish public schools in an under-served and under-resourced school district. As a consequence of their work and a long-term relationship with the city and district, municipal officials often expedite building permit requests through the bureaucracy of approvals and the

22. "William Wilberforce," http://abolition.e2bn.org/people_24.html.

schools provide storage space for the nonprofit's equipment on their property. There is no obligation on the part of the receiving school to participate in any faith activities to receive this benefit. But the city and the school district have blurred the lines of separation of church and state in order to better serve the students and teachers of this school district. I will say more about these kinds of programs in the final chapter by highlighting a few stories that capture what it means to recover the church's first-word impulse and channel its energy and hope toward this kind of work as it engages in politics.

This prophetic and creative role of religious communities plays an important part in contributing to the development of a robust democratic tradition. It captures two sentiments found in the Gospel of Mark when Jesus is asked about paying taxes. In the text, it is clear that the question posed to Jesus of whether to pay taxes to Caesar is a thinly veiled attempt to trap him inside a particular ideology and draw boundary lines of where Jesus fits in the different Jewish perspectives on Rome.

In Mark 12:13–17, Jesus is asked about paying taxes to Caesar: "Is it lawful to pay taxes to the emperor or not?" Jesus reminds them of their commitments "elsewhere" by referring to the image on the coin: "Whose head is this, and whose title?" Like most national currency, the leader or past leader's image is on the coin, so they answered, "The emperor's." Jesus poignant response, "Give to the emperor the things that are the emperor's, and to God the things that are God's," reminds them that there are commitments outside of government that take precedent over the limited work that any institution is trying to accomplish. The reference to the image on the coin had a subtext anchored in the Genesis story in the Pentateuch: humanity was created in the image of God. If Caesar's image is stamped on the currency, God's image is stamped on all of creation. Therefore, all of life is to be given to God, while participation in government is only one aspect of a broader view of what it means to be human in the world. This creates the tension that Rorty wants to avoid—religious citizens have commitments elsewhere. But it is those commitments that can challenge the drift or tyranny of the majority.

In a similar fashion, when asked about leadership in the kingdom of God, Jesus again gives a counter-cultural response. Mark 10:41–45 is Jesus' response to James's and John's request to sit in places of prominence and authority in anticipation of their hope that Jesus would establish a messianic reign in Israel. Of course, the other disciples were aghast at this request, and

Jesus had to remind them all that his way of leadership and authority was different than what they observed in the world, and that it differed from the way that most in the Jewish community were relating to the hegemony of Rome:

> You know that among the Gentiles those whom they recognize as their rulers lord it over them, and their great ones are tyrants over them. But it is not so among you: but whoever wishes to become great among you must be your servant, and whoever wishes to be first among you must be slave of all. For the Son of Man did not come to be served but to serve, and to give his life a ransom for many.

Service to others was supposed to be a mark of genuine faithfulness to Christ. This creates space for Christian citizens in any form of government to turn their attention to the needs of the community and love people in creative, concrete, and sacrificial ways.

The final way that religion can complement democracy is in the development of supererogatory virtue—that is, virtue that goes beyond the requirements of the democratic tradition. One of the strengths of the democratic tradition is in its ability to accommodate a pluralistic public square. By necessity, it has to maintain a thin ethic of "harm" to allow for so many competing visions of the good life: do not harm others, do not harm society, and do not harm oneself (although this last "harm principle" is rarely legislated). It has three other virtues that accompany this ethic of harm: (1) putting structures in place to limit its own power; (2) allowing for (and hopefully encouraging) a variety of secondary associations that make up "civil society"—the informal structures that fill in the gaps that any kind of government produces; and (3) creating space for a robust conversation about the goods of society and how those goods get distributed justly. Again, Rorty captures the virtues of the democratic tradition succinctly and engagingly—democracies broaden the range of social justice—the inclusion of an ever-widening group of people able to define their own happiness without interference or oppression of others. Civil society then, constantly widens to include more and more possibilities for human happiness.[23]

Rorty argues that religious virtues contradict these democratic virtues. Therefore, he advocates leaving religion and the virtues it requires behind—as a relic of the past—so that we can become the kind of persons who can maximize the freedoms of others by eliminating an external frame

---

23. Rorty, *Achieving Our Country*, 31.

of reference: God. This is a human endeavor that has more possibilities for hope if an external frame of reference that limits human freedoms is removed. Human beings hold the hope for progress in society.[24] Echoing Walt Whitman, Rorty thinks of democracy as a poetic experiment in national self-creation—an elevation of human essence to the place that God once occupied. William James spoke of democracy as "a kind of religion," and John Dewey saw it as "a metaphysics of the relation of man and his experience in nature."[25] For Rorty, the American democratic project is a unique opportunity to develop and sustain a form of social organization that does not depend on anything outside of references to human possibility to determine a moral good:

> So much for my interpretation of Whitman's and Dewey's attempts thoroughly to secularize America—to see America as the paradigmatic democracy, and thus as the country which would pride itself as one in which governments and social institutions exist only for the purpose of making a new sort of individual possible, one who will take nothing as authoritative save free consensus between as diverse a variety of citizens as can possibly be produced.[26]

In a thoroughly secular democracy, a different kind of religion is necessary in order to completely sanitize the public square, and scholars must try to instill into the democratic tradition a mystical sense of virtue and texture. But why not just tap into the resources that are already present in the religious traditions that make up civil society?

What I think that most want to avoid is what Scotty McLennan describes as "intolerant, hurtful, oppressive, and abusive" forms of Christianity, which can be generalized to all religious traditions.[27] Rorty is specifically worried about the ecclesiastical structures that make statements about orthodox belief and practice. In chapter 4 I will make a case that Christianity specifically (and religion in general) needs a complement when it is the dominant tradition in a particular culture so that it can avoid these very characterizations that come with a quick survey of church history. But as the title of Martin Thielen's book suggests, *The Answer to Bad Religion is not No Religion*.[28] There is an alternative to dismissing religion altogether

24. Rorty, *Philosophy and Social Hope*, 265.

25. Rorty, *Achieving Our Country*, 18.

26. Ibid., 30.

27. McLennan, *Christ for Unitarian Universalists*, 13.

28. Thielen, *Answer to Bad Religion*.

in Thielen's conclusion; the answer to the intolerant, hurtful, and abusive forms of religion (Christianity specifically in my case) is "good religion." But what does "good religion" look like, and what can Christian virtue contribute as a complement to the democratic tradition?

Here, let us contrast the core virtue of democracy (preventing harm) with the core virtue of Christian faith: love. As I stated above, harm is a minimalist ethic; it is legislated when it occurs. It is generally self-focused—when am I (or my community) being harmed? And, as much as it accommodates pluralism, I am not sure that it encourages pluralism—we often define the "other" as a potential candidate for harming us. That is, when it comes to legislation, we tend to focus on what impacts us most and then secondarily what might impact others. However, the Christian virtue of love, especially *agape* or unconditional love, pushes us to consider those that exist outside of our natural range of moral concern. This kind of love is a supererogatory virtue that requires more than just toleration, but a care and concern for the other. Love is a difficult virtue to define specifically because everyone imports meaning into that term. But it takes on a certain kind of quality in the Christian tradition reflected in the teachings and stories of Jesus in the Gospels; and how the writers of the letters of the New Testament reflect back on the meaning of the words and actions of Jesus for the nascent communities that are forming in various cities around the Roman Empire.

The starting point for any definition of Christian love is Jesus' reaffirmation of the Hebrew Scriptures' double-love command: "'You shall love the Lord your God with all your heart, and with all your soul, and with all your mind.' This is the greatest and first commandment. And a second is like it: 'You shall love your neighbor as yourself.' On these two commandments hang all the law and the prophets" (Matt 22:37–40). When pressed further to define one's neighbor in a parallel passage in Luke, Jesus tells the story of the Good Samaritan (Luke 10:25–37). Love extends our boundaries of moral concern toward others who we might not consider included in our moral obligations. In the Gospel of John, Jesus is recorded as saying this to his disciples about love: "Greater love has no man than this, that a man lay down his life for his friends" (John 15:13). The letters of the New Testament continue this theme: "While we were still weak, at the right time Christ died for the ungodly. Why, one will hardly die for a righteous man—though perhaps for a good man one will dare even to die. But God shows his love for us in that while we were yet sinners Christ died for us" (Rom 5:6–8).

And in Philippians 2:4–5: "Let each of us look not to your own interests but to the interest of others. Let the same mind be in you that was in Christ Jesus." Finally, the great treatise on love is in 1 Corinthians 13:4–8a: "Love is patient; love is kind; love is not envious or boastful or arrogant or rude. It does not insist on its own way; it is not irritable or resentful; it does not rejoice in wrongdoing, but rejoices in the truth. It bears all things, believes all things, hopes all things, endures all things. Love never ends."

This kind of virtue is not required in the democratic tradition—it goes beyond the requirements and virtues of the tradition. We need citizens who are cultivating other virtues that can help carry democracy forward. The Christian tradition's notion of love (at its best) includes an "other-centered-ness" that can complement the democratic tradition's ethic of harm.

This idea of a complement can be seen in the essence of Michael Walzer's work in his book *Revolution of the Saints.*[29] In it, he argues that the Christian tradition helped to provide a theological framework for the rise of the democratic tradition. I have already outlined some of the major beliefs that created analogies that are embedded in the democratic tradition: the reality of sin and the need for checks and balances; the priesthood of all believers and the right for everyone to have a say in how they are governed (not just the elites); a loyalty to Christ above all other loyalties that became the impetus for the presence of secondary associations. Further, Walzer argues that the Puritan metaphor of "the ship of state" encouraged passionate involvement in the state and the possibility of dissent if the ship was sinking. This was the creative stimulus that was particularly suited for the upheaval and transitions that seventeenth-century England was going through to become a democratic state. Christianity and democracy seem well-suited to complement one another as we look at history. I am not making an argument that other religious traditions are not as equipped to be that same kind of qualitative complement—that is an argument that they can take up, but Christianity and democracy have had close ties throughout the development of Western culture.

There is a caution here as I argue for opening the public conversation to religious citizens without constraints on their reasons or language—we have a history where Christianity has sometimes overstepped its boundaries. I am not arguing to eliminate the two frames of separation of church and state. I am arguing for the possibility of a blurring inside those frames that at its most creative might become an artful way to address our most

29. Walzer, *Revolution of the Saints.*

pressing social problems. In the next chapter, I want to address this worry a bit more head-on and argue that Christianity, because it has been the dominant religious tradition in the West since the fourth century, needs a complement as well. And the democratic tradition has sharpened the Christian tradition in that way by always advocating for the inclusion of more people in the goods of society.

4

Christianity Might Need a Complement

IN CHAPTER 3, I argued that the democratic tradition necessitates a complementary tradition to produce the virtue that it needs to continue forward.
Its thin ethic that can accommodate variegated secondary associations in
society has difficulty cultivating the kind of virtue necessary for its own
maintenance and survival. As the cacophony of voices in the public square
only increases and the heterogeneity of moral perspectives exacerbates a
shrinking consensus, democracy needs something to counter the devolu-
tion to pure power as a way to establish a community's moral good. My
contention is that democracy might collapse in on itself as more groups
struggle to reach for power. I have tried to note how democracy and
Christian faith have historically traveled together in the West, and that they
have contributed to some of the West's great moral achievements. There is
reason to think that this is more than just a historical coincidence. These
two traditions may be uniquely suited to complement one another. What I
am not arguing is that this complementary tradition has to necessarily be
Christianity, or religion per se; but the Christian virtue of supererogatory
love counterbalances the democratic tradition's thin ethic of harm. Further,
I tried to argue that the "otherness" of religious traditions in general give
religion a unique prophetic voice as the winds of social consensus blow
inconsistently. In this chapter, I want to explore the connection between
democracy and Christianity in the reverse direction: how the democratic
tradition can make the Christian tradition stronger and more robust. I
will argue that the democratic ideal of providing the most goods for the
most people has had a prophetic role in the development of the Christian

tradition in the West. The complementary relationship between these two traditions runs in both directions.

In contrast to democracy's thin ethic, the Christian tradition is replete with thickness and particularity. This particularity is necessarily exclusive—to define oneself and one's tradition in specific ways is to simultaneously define an "other." When a thick religious tradition like Christianity becomes hegemonic in culture, its absolutism can become marginalizing in a different way than democracy's majority. And on occasion, it can become oppressive. It needs a prophetic voice to draw attention to that "other"—especially when their voices are heard less often because their ethic may run in the opposite direction of a Christian ethic. Michael Walzer draws a parallel conclusion with Judaism when the Israelites asked for a king in their early formation as a nation (1 Sam 8). Walzer argues that when the monarchy was established in Israel, the office of prophet also emerged. The role of the prophet was to remind the king that they were a steward of what God was doing and a servant to the people.[1] It was often a lonely and difficult job when the prophet's words cut across the king's assertion of power. Prophets are often internal to a tradition; they understand the language and moral framework and challenge those in power to be faithful to the first principles, beliefs, texts, and way of rational inquiry. But prophets can also come from the outside—challenging the powerful because they can see and empathize with those that are consistently left out of the just distribution of the "good."

Christianity is a stand-alone tradition; it does not affirm a particular form of government. As I argued in chapter 2, it is an international community that exists in the contexts of socialist, communist, democratic, and even Sharia-Law forms of government. It has a thin ethic in relationship to the office of government (Rom 13; 1 Pet 2), one that is less than the current emphasis on politics of many in the evangelical community. The kingdom of God was not to be established through political means, but through the faithful work of the church in reliance on and cooperation with God. The church is a politic unto itself, and only secondarily political in the world's manner. The muddled relationship that developed out of the marriage of the church and Rome shifted the focus of the church from being culturally nonconformist to becoming the caretakers of culture. Martin Luther King Jr. captured this in his sermons during the Civil Rights Movement: "'Do not conform' is difficult advice in a generation when crowd pressures have

---

1. Walzer, *In God's Shadow*, 86.

unconsciously conditioned our minds and feet to move to the rhythmic drumbeat of the status quo. In spite of this prevailing tendency to conform, we as Christians have a mandate to be noncomformists."[2] As in Walzer's argument about how the office of prophet developed within the monarchy of Judaism, some kind of voice is necessary to challenge the tendency of those Christians who hold some cultural power to conserve that power. This is also John H. Yoder's critique of Western Christendom: that Christianity lost its creative and prophetic edge when it was baptized into power.

Yoder draws from his extensive experience arguing for Christian nonviolence in the face of wars. He maintains that when you are not allowed to consider violence as a way to settle disputes, you are forced to come up with different alternatives and more creative solutions when resolving conflict than by going to war.[3] The possibility of mutually assured destruction is not a strategy for peace that the church utilizes. Similarly, and analogically, if one does not consider legislative power as the primary means to inculcate a moral vision of the good life, one might work to come up with more creative solutions to society's most pressing problems. So my contention is this: the particularity of religion needs the prophetic cry of those on the "outside" for more rights. Pluralism goads religion into a more authentic expression of itself as the church considers the epistemological challenges and the crises that those challenges create as a result of being involved in a pluralistic public square. As I argued earlier, a thick tradition (Christianity included) needs these crises to mature. Fundamentalism happens in any tradition when it will not consider these challenges and only falls back on a simplistic affirmation of its founding beliefs, texts, and authorities.

I want to highlight three ways in which the democratic tradition has complemented the Christian tradition in its unique relationship in Western culture. First, a pluralistic public square draws out religious language, religious reasons, and religious motives. It puts them into plain sight. That is why I think that secularists' attempts to sanitize the public square are wrong-headed; allowing religious language into the public conversation means that religious people hear their reasons "out loud." They see the response of non-adherents of their particular religious tradition, and it allows their sacred texts to be challenged by different perspectives (including the primary sources of authority of the Enlightenment: reason, experience, and science). With the advent of social media, the feedback can sometimes

2. King, *Strength to Love*, 21.
3. Yoder et al., *War of the Lamb*, 13.

be immediate. Even if a religious person does not change his or her view on a particular social or legislative issue, it may become more nuanced, strengthened, or settled because of the sharpening effect that is created when interacting with people who hold and argue for contrary views.

Second, when particular religious traditions become hegemonic in culture, they tend to try to conserve their position of power. This is especially true of absolutist religions that have an external frame of reference. When citizens equate their good with God's good, their moral argument comes with more force. I argued that this is a good thing when it comes to moral staying power and the ability to not drift with cultural currents, but it is not good on a conservative basis alone. Christians especially should be careful equating their good with God's intentions. The Christian doctrines of human finiteness (we are limited in our knowledge) and human depravity (we tend to bend the "long arc of the moral universe" in our direction) and the consistent appeals to humility in the Christian Scriptures should all contribute to an air of caution. Again, discerning which moral positions should be held onto despite opposition and which are just cultural expressions is an important part of what it means to become mature in the faith in the Christian tradition.

The third way that democracy has a prophetic voice to Christianity is in the development of empathy for others. This seems counterintuitive given the admonitions of Jesus to pay attention "to the least of these" (Matt 25). But while democracies necessarily marginalize, ideally they also invite those on the margins into conversation and give them a vehicle to argue for their rights. To hear other religious reasons, to imagine what it would be like if another religious tradition had the same power and majority that you have, and to hear the "voices that have been excluded," the injustice that they have experienced, and any oppression that they face should soften the conserving tendencies of particularist religious traditions. I argued in chapter 3 that democracies marginalize by appealing to the majority. Here I am arguing that all traditions marginalize in some way—they create an "other" by defining their particularities. So, all traditions need some kind of prophetic word from the outside to pay attention to those that they marginalize—but Christianity as a tradition should welcome these challenges because they fit squarely with the teachings of Jesus and the ethos of the early church.

Let's take each of these complements and explore them further. The idea that opening the public square to religious reasons, language, and motives seems to be an anathema to those that hold a tight perspective on the separation of church and state. The goal is to keep the public square free of religion altogether. I maintained earlier that this cleaning up of the public square unnecessarily privileges non-religious reasons, motives, and actions. It implies that these reasons are neutral and unbiased. There may have been a time in the history of Western democracy where this was necessary because non-religious citizens were being marginalized by the dominant Christian spirit of the day, but this hardly seems to be the case any longer. How do we move past this overcorrection? As long as all religious reasons are allowed into the public square, or enough diversity is present to be somewhat representative of the various religious traditions that hold a stake in a particular good and the impact that it might have on them, we can include religious reasons and voices on their own terms—give them agency in the public conversation without predetermining the limits of that agency. With enough representation, we can avoid the establishment of any one particular religion that Jefferson was worried about. We do not have to exclude all of religion to prevent establishment—we just try to be careful so that one religion does not become hegemonic over all others.

One place where this first prophetic relationship between democracy and Christianity is currently happening is in our cultural arguments over same-sex marriage. I have talked some about the cultural revolution of the 1960s and how that was the social outworking of the postmodern intellectual challenge to metanarratives. Why should one community's version of rationality, morality, and culture subsume other communities under their story? Each community has a story to tell. The most obvious in the 1960s was the Civil Rights Movement—why should blacks have their story told by whites; or Africans by Europeans? But there were other stories to hear as we recovered the voices from long-overlooked minorities in culture. Why should women have their stories told by men? Why should Eastern cultures have their stories told by people from the West? Why should the LGBTQ community have their stories told by the straight community?

The gay rights movement was birthed out of the Civil Rights Movement. The LGBTQ community (I will use this as the accepted shorthand for a wide range of sexual minorities that have had their stories told by heterosexuals) recognized a parallel with the black community in the basic lack of fundamental rights that heterosexuals assumed. Gays and lesbians were frequently denied housing, jobs, and health care because of their sexual orientation—and sometimes still are. (In certain cities—Kutztown,

Pennsylvania, for example—there is no law barring landlords from discriminating against renters on the basis of sexual orientation.[4]) What started with the Stonewall Riots in 1969 during the back end of the Civil Rights Movement gathered momentum over time and resulted in Massachusetts passing a law in 2004 that allowed same-sex couples marriage rights. This created a firestorm in the conservative religious communities. They lamented the familiar story of the decline of American Christian values and the promotion of the "homosexual agenda." Emboldened by a new front opened up in the culture wars, conservative evangelicals took to the public square to argue against the notion that same-sex couples could infringe on the rights of heterosexual married couples, and that marriage was sacred and includes only monogamous heterosexual couples who enter into lifelong covenants. This is an important prophetic moment because it brought Christian marriage into the center of the public conversation. In this case, the democratic tradition and its focus on rights created space for the LGBTQ community to ask and argue for marriage rights. It also prophetically challenged the Christian tradition's theology and practice of marriage. As the public conversation escalated, this exposed several difficult places where Christianity had veered from faithfulness in their family ethic.

A common challenge extended to conservative evangelicals is that the church has readily accommodated divorce, but has failed to include LGBTQ persons. People in the pews of churches participate in pornography, but stereotype LGBTQ with pejorative quips like "the gay lifestyle" or "God made Adam and Eve, not Adam and Steve." There is a lot of research on the success or failure of Christian marriage in America. Much has been made about the 50 percent divorce rate and that Christians divorce at roughly the same rate as those that do not identify with the Christian tradition. The most nuanced statistics do demonstrate that divorce is a problem in the church, but they seem to indicate that if you are an active Christian Protestant or an active Catholic, your chances of divorce are about one-third less likely.[5] This is roughly true about pornography use as well; according to the Barna Research Group, Christians are about three times less likely to

4. Segarra, "In Pennsylvania," http://www.newsworks.org/index.php/local/keystone-crossroads/89250-in-most-of-pennsylvania-its-legal-to-deny-someone-housing-for-being-gay-lesbian-bisexual-or-transgender.

5. Stetzer, "Marriage, Divorce, and the Church," http://www.christianitytoday.com/edstetzer/2014/february/marriage-divorce-and-body-of-christ-what-do-stats-say-and-c.html.

view pornography than others. So there is some statistical evidence that an active Christian faith is a distinguishing marker for the success of a marriage. But the pseudo-documentary film, *For the Bible Tells Me So*, opens with fundamentalist preachers railing against gays and lesbians in a way that demonstrates the harsh language and strong negative rhetoric aimed at people with a non-heterosexual orientation.[6] The film also asks "Christians on the street" what the Bible has to say about homosexuality and it reveals that most non-professional Christian judgments on this important moral and theological issue are culturally inherited and not significantly thought through.

My point here is that the question of the rights of gays and lesbians to marry has pushed the non-fundamentalist, but conservative Christians to take a closer look at their sacred texts on the topic of sexuality in general and same-sex questions specifically. It has nudged conservative Christians to reconsider previously held assumptions and prejudices toward the LGBTQ community and inspired new openings for confession, repentance and for dialogue (Andrew Marin, who founded The Marin Foundation, is an example of a conservative Christian who is trying to create a different kind of dialogue between people of faith and the LGBTQ community).[7] The LGBTQ community has prophetically challenged Christians to consider what the Christian Scriptures teach about sexuality, marriage, and family that might distinguish it from the surrounding culture. And finally, it has provoked them to consider what kind of socially conferred rights might be good for same-sex couples. There has been some movement in all of these areas. Some Christians have changed their view of what the Bible says about same-sex sexuality (such as Tony Compolo or Nicholas Wolterstorff),[8] some evangelical churches have come out as affirming same-sex relationships (such as City Church in San Francisco),[9] some have drawn on the models developed in European countries and argue that churches should stop acting as agents of the state and get out of the wedding business altogether. They separate the sacred ceremony of marriage in the church from the state's ability to grant marriage licenses. Finally, others have maintained that, in a pluralistic culture, marriage rights should be conferred

6. Karslake, *For the Bible Tells Me So*.

7. See the Marin Foundation website at http://www.themarinfoundation.org/.

8. Campolo, "For the Record," http://tonycampolo.org/for-the-record-tony-campolo-releases-a-new-statement/#.WHGPRDu7pSU.

9. Harrell, "A Letter from the Elder Board," https://www.citychurchsf.org/A-Letter-From-The-Elder-Board.

to same-sex couples while still holding traditional theological views. The point of this is not an affirmation of either side of this hotly contested conversation over same-sex marriage—it is to show the prophetic role that democracy has played for Christianity when a conversation becomes public, and the wide range of responses that it has opened as the Christian tradition wrestles with this challenge.

A second way that democracy has played a prophetic role in strengthening the Christian tradition is its challenge to the assumption that Christians have a corner on the American heritage and therefore should remain in privileged positions of power. As America (and the West more generally) continues to become more diverse ethnically, culturally, and religiously, the question of who has the dominant voice in the public square should remain open. I argued in chapter 1 that Stanley Hauerwas maintains that this very notion of having a culturally privileged position has compromised the faithfulness and distinctiveness of the church. It has washed out the uniqueness of the Christian tradition in favor of a more "civil religion." For Hauerwas, this is a loss of Christianity altogether: "the church's social task is first of all its willingness to be a community formed by a language that the world does not share."[10] He argues that the Christian church needs to recover its distinctiveness as a community "in the world but not of the world"—resident aliens in whatever culture followers of Christ find themselves in.[11] If Richard Rorty wants to maintain a "pure" democratic tradition based solely on secular arguments, Hauerwas shares a parallel concern for the Christian tradition. For Hauerwas, Christianity is adulterated by trying to conserve a Christendom that washes out the particularities of what it means to be followers of Jesus in favor of a more generalized public Christian ethic.

Hauerwas's efforts to reclaim the "countercultural social structure of the church," does not mean a complete withdrawal from the world. Rather, any involvement in affirming what the world is doing is a "proclamatory action" and witness.[12] He can affirm a kind of "radical democracy" that pays attention to the edges of the democratic tradition because it localizes the moral language and gives it meaning again. In his early work, Hauerwas tried to avoid terms like "love" and "justice" when he spoke about ethics and morality, because they had lost their meaning—the universalizing attempts to take the Christian meaning of these terms and apply them to

10. Hauerwas, *Against the Nations*, 11.
11. Hauerwas and Willimon, *Resident Aliens*.
12. Ibid., 46.

a wider segment of society stripped them of their depth. His book titles reflected this position, *Resident Aliens, Against the Nations,* etc . . . and he was criticized for being sectarian and obscurantist. He was also criticized because, by giving up the language of "love" and "justice," he had handed over these terms to the secularists when they had deep Judeo-Christian roots. But in his later work, he tries to blunt those criticisms by demonstrating how the distinctive *polis* of the church can contribute to radical democracy. Hauerwas uses the term "radical democracy" to portray the kind of local democracies that have moral meaning. He bristles at the idea that Christianity and democracy (as a larger ideology) have any kind of redeeming relationship.

Further, Hauerwas sees the same prophetic role that democracy can play in the Christian tradition for which I have been arguing. Because the slow, painstaking process of politics is always local, and the church's expression of faithfulness to Jesus is also bounded by that locality (expressions of faithfulness to Christ are always culturally conditioned), the church can learn from radical democracy. The internal conflict that is necessary for growth is sparked by having to grapple with the localized language of the political. This is the way that democracy makes the Christian tradition sharper and more robust. Here again, Hauerwas parallels Rorty. Rorty argues that the problem with religion is not the localized parish-level efforts of a congregation to contribute to the good of the community; rather, it is the larger denominational and ecclesial organization of the church that makes pronouncements of orthodox moral behavior that limits human happiness.[13] Similarly, Hauerwas argues that local-level democracy—radical democracy—has moral language that is rich with meaning; it is when we begin to talk about democracy as an ideology that the meaning of moral language gets lost.

He goes on to argue that the church cannot control its conversation partners and how they use moral language. At every turn, the Christian tradition faces questions from the edges of radical democracy. He calls the church's response to these questions a "semi-permeable orthodoxy." He defines orthodoxy as the "developments across time that the church has found necessary for keeping the story of Jesus straight."[14] This resonates with MacIntyre's definition of a tradition—a narrative that extends through time that has survived its epistemological challenges. For Hauerwas, the

13. Rorty, "Religion in the Public Square," 143.
14. Hauerwas and Coles, *Christianity, Democracy,* 30.

church can learn from radical democracy that the answers to the challenges of orthodoxy should not be predetermined beforehand and our illocutionary partners cannot be pre-selected in order to preserve the purity of our tradition.

The third way that the democratic tradition can be a prophetic witness to the Christian tradition is by putting Christianity in proximity with other stories. My friend Reggie Williams argues that it was this "walking with another" that was the catalyst for Dietrich Bonhoeffer's shift from German Nationalism to Jewish sympathizer. In his book *Bonhoeffer's Black Jesus*, Williams argues that Bonhoeffer's year in America—when he studied at Union Theological Seminary—impacted his views toward the Jewish community in Germany and Europe. Williams goes on to show that it was not necessarily Bonhoeffer's courses at Union, but his internship at Abyssinian Baptist Church, that challenged his faith. At the time, Abyssinian Baptist was one of the largest churches in America, experiencing momentous growth and having a substantial influence in New York City. They were a growing congregation during the peak of the Harlem Renaissance. Harlem was becoming a center for the post-reconstruction black community's hopes for redefining itself apart from slavery. The music, art, and religion in Harlem reflected the move away from a Christian faith that had been dominated by white slave-owning males of European descent for an expression of those that found Christ during their suffering in slavery. For some, this meant moving away from Christianity altogether, but for others, Christian faith took on new meanings.[15]

In this mix of different Christian and cultural expressions of "blackness" in New York, Bonhoeffer heard the stories of the suffering of blacks under the dominant power of majority culture, the co-option of Christ to serve those in power, and the reimagining of Christian faith for those on the margins. He also experienced the depth of preaching, worship, and fellowship of the black parishioners at Abyssinian Baptist. Williams maintains that this proximity to the African-American community in Harlem engendered an empathy that Bonhoeffer then transferred to the Jewish community when he returned to Germany. Bonhoeffer would eventually be martyred for his participation in the resistance just days before the liberation of German concentration camps by the allies. Experiencing those particular stories in Harlem was the catalyst for a kind of faith that we now study for its moral prescience. Even theologian Karl Barth, the architect of

15. Williams, *Bonhoeffer's Black Jesus*.

the Confessing Church and the Barmen Declaration, said that he wished he would have seen the "Nazi problem" as early as Bonhoeffer did.

Another way that empathy is built is through storytelling. When we tell our story and listen to the stories of others, we can see our common interests and struggles. Democracy, by its very nature, puts us into contact with other people and their stories. Let me give two examples, one historical and one current of how a story can change a person's ethic. During World War II, the small village of Le Chambon, France is said to have saved or protected more than five thousand Jews from the Nazi pogrom. In his documentary *Weapons of the Spirit*, Peter Sauvage takes a film crew to the village in the early 1980s in order to interview those who participated in the resistance.[16] He was a Jew, born during the war, and he became a recipient of the generosity of the "Chambonaise." He wanted to return to help tell the stories of those who participated in the resistance. He also wanted to discover if there were any common threads that might be helpful in understanding why this little village stood out among its European counterparts. Apart from their credulity at the question: their most common answer was "why wouldn't we do this?" it became apparent that the villagers' history of religious persecution played a large part in developing empathy for the Jewish community. Many of the residents of Le Chambon were descendants of the Heugenots, a Protestant community that suffered under Catholic persecution in France in the sixteenth and seventeenth centuries.[17] The stories of suffering were told through several generations in a manner that produced a different way of seeing religious minorities in their midst. While Le Chambon was predominantly Protestant during the early twentieth century, they coexisted peacefully with both Catholics and Jews in their village. Because they had a narrative as a religious minority, they viewed other religious minorities differently (with empathy). This created a category of care that motivated efforts to resist the Nazi's attempts to deport the Jews in France. Le Chambon also became a center for the publishing of false identity papers so that Jews could travel across European borders without being captured. This little community had a powerful impact on others because of the stories that were a part of their history.

A current example of how stories impact empathy is Christian philosopher Nicholas Wolterstorff's recent lecture that affirmed that same-sex couples can fit squarely into Christian orthodoxy. As Wolterstorff describes

16. Sauvage, *Weapons of the Spirit*.
17. Sunshine, *Reforming French Protestantism*.

it, one of his reasons for shifting from two thousand years of sexual ortho-doxy was because of the stories he heard: "I've listened to these people. To their agony. To their feelings of exclusion and oppression. To their long-ings. To their expressions of love. To their commitments. To their faith. So listening has changed me."[18] Whether you agree with Wolterstorff or not on this particular issue, the point is clear: hearing people's stories builds relationship and relationship produces empathy. It is easy to stand outside of a community and pass moral judgment on the behavior that does not match your own expectations of what is right. It is far more difficult when you move into a community, take on their language and develop relation-ships with the very people with whom you disagree. This is the existential challenge of a public faith that is put into proximity to other community's stories.

What I've tried to say in this chapter is that the democratic tradition has had a prophetic voice in the sharpening of the Christian tradition in the West. When religious people hear their reasons out loud and see how people who do not share their same basic convictions respond, when they are challenged to consider the rights of those who have suffered injustice, and when they hear the stories of people from other traditions it forces them to reexamine their beliefs, texts, and authorities and this can produce a more faithful Christian tradition. Their moral conclusions may not al-ways change (the progressive assumption is that time and relationship will cause someone to match your moral expectations) but they will be more thoughtful, more supported, more meaningful, and more empathetic.

If I can gather the arguments from the last two chapters together, I am arguing for an open public square with the accepted boundary conditions of (1) freedom of religion and (2) coercive power being held only by le-gitimate governmental institutions (the non-establishment clause). Within these two conditions, the relationship between church and state should in-clude both religious language and religious activities that contribute to the "good" of society without any obligation of "conversion" or "participation." The temptation to make strong demarcations of separation beyond these two boundary conditions actually weakens religious traditions and weak-ens the democratic tradition because they are missing the prophetic edges that strengthen each other. I am arguing for a "blur" in the space between these two boundaries. In chapter 1, I call this the "art of pluralism." And I

18. Findlay, "Wolterstorff Says 'Yes,'" http://www.calvin.edu/chimes/2016/10/22/wolterstorff-says-yes-to-same-sex-marriage/.

maintain that the great examples of moral progress in the last two centuries have resulted from the tension created by this blur. President Lincoln's work in abolishing slavery and Dr. Martin Luther King Jr.'s work in the Civil Rights Movement are examples of how religious language and democratic language together were used to call America to be more faithful to its promises as a country. The body of Lincolns's second inaugural address called for a theological understanding of the war and the mercy to move forward in reconstruction. It offered a hope for the future that included both North and South in a unified America. I quote it at length because of the theological framework that Lincoln used:

> One-eighth of the whole population were colored slaves, not distributed generally over the Union, but localized in the southern part of it. These slaves constituted a peculiar and powerful interest. All knew that this interest was somehow the cause of the war. To strengthen, perpetuate, and extend this interest was the object for which the insurgents would rend the Union even by war, while the Government claimed no right to do more than to restrict the territorial enlargement of it. Neither party expected for the war the magnitude or the duration which it has already attained. Neither anticipated that the cause of the conflict might cease with or even before the conflict itself should cease. Each looked for an easier triumph, and a result less fundamental and astounding. Both read the same Bible and pray to the same God, and each invokes His aid against the other. It may seem strange that any men should dare to ask a just God's assistance in wringing their bread from the sweat of other men's faces, but let us judge not, that we be not judged. The prayers of both could not be answered. That of neither has been answered fully. The Almighty has His own purposes. "Woe unto the world because of offenses; for it must needs be that offenses come, but woe to that man by whom the offense cometh." If we shall suppose that American slavery is one of those offenses which, in the providence of God, must needs come, but which, having continued through His appointed time, He now wills to remove, and that He gives to both North and South this terrible war as the woe due to those by whom the offense came, shall we discern therein any departure from those divine attributes which the believers in a living God always ascribe to Him? Fondly do we hope, fervently do we pray, that this mighty scourge of war may speedily pass away. Yet, if God wills that it continue until all the wealth piled by the bondsman's two hundred and fifty years of unrequited toil shall be sunk, and until every drop of blood drawn with the lash shall be paid by another drawn with the sword, as

was said three thousand years ago, so still it must be said "the judgments of the Lord are true and righteous altogether."

With malice toward none, with charity for all, with firmness in the right as God gives us to see the right, let us strive on to finish the work we are in, to bind up the nation's wounds, to care for him who shall have borne the battle and for his widow and his orphan, to do all which may achieve and cherish a just and lasting peace among ourselves and with all nations.[19]

Similarly, Martin Luther King Jr.'s speech at the Washington Mall during the Civil Rights Movement appealed to theological and democratic principles to call America to fulfill its promises to all its citizens. Here are a few poignant and familiar lines that illustrate this point:

Now is the time to make justice a reality for all of God's children. It would be fatal for the nation to overlook the urgency of the moment. . . . No, no, we are not satisfied, and we will not be satisfied until justice rolls down like waters and righteousness like a mighty stream. . . . we will be able to speed up that day when all of God's children, black men and white men, Jews and Gentiles, Protestants and Catholics, will be able to join hands and sing in the words of the old Negro spiritual, "Free at last, Free at last, Great God a-mighty, We are free at last."[20]

Here we have two examples of the blur that I am describing at the prophetic edges of religion and democracy that contributed to moral progress and challenged democracy and Christianity to be more faithful to their respective traditions.

If this is the case and my thesis is correct, then two corollaries follow: first, those in governmental institutions have an obligation to learn the language of the particular religious traditions of their constituents. A failure to be competent in understanding religion only marginalizes religious citizens. After the horrific tragedy of September 11th, 2001 in America, president George W. Bush gave a speech calling for a "crusade" against the terrorists. That language effectively lumped the Muslim-American community into the acts of terrorists and recapitulated old tensions between Christians and Muslims throughout the world. The history of the Crusades is a long and violent conflict between Christians and Muslims that carries scars today,

19. Lincoln, "Second Inaugural Address," http://avalon.law.yale.edu/19th_century/lincoln2.asp.

20. King, "I Have a Dream," http://www.thekingcenter.org/archive/document/i-have-dream-1.

and many American Muslims felt marginalized by President Bush's words. Similarly, in 2008, then-presidential candidate Barack Obama visited one of Evangelicalism's most famous churches—Saddleback Church in Orange County, California. Rick Warren, author of the *New York Times* best seller *The Purpose Driven Life*, is the pastor of Saddleback. Warren asked Obama about his position on the contentious issue of abortion—one of Evangelicalism's most important social concerns. Obama responded by saying that some of the concerns of the religious are "above his pay grade" and deferred to the democratic party's platform.[21] He quickly retracted his statement, recognizing that this trivialized an important issue to a significant number of Americans. The inability to understand and converse in religious language is a deficit for those who hold positions of power in a democracy.

The second corollary is that particular religious traditions—and here I will focus on my own tradition, evangelical Christianity—have the obligation to love their neighbors by learning their language. The double-love command—to love God and love our neighbor as ourselves—means that, if Christians ask governmental leaders to learn religious language, then we have an obligation to learn others' language as well. This includes learning ways to put theological language into terms that others can understand. There cannot be a demand that others learn our language without the obligation to learn theirs as well.

Another way to love one's neighbors is to not coerce them. I will talk about this more in chapter 5. If a particular position in the Christian tradition is not affirmed or legislated in the public square, the Christian tradition has an alternative to legislative coercion: as a standalone tradition, they can model moral good to the surrounding community. Christian moral precepts are primarily for the community of faith that calls Jesus Lord and only secondarily for the wider community. They were meant to be adopted, not legislated: recognized from the ground up as a way to experience a meaningful and significant life and a demonstration of the "wisdom of God," not legislated from the top down so society can become more Christian. Finally, another way to love one's neighbors is to initiate efforts that seek the welfare of the community. That is, noticing the needs of the community and mobilizing small efforts to begin to meet those needs. I will highlight some examples of this in chapter 6. It is at this point that we need to bring the argument of this book together to set a trajectory for a way forward in negotiating the boundaries between religion and democracy.

21. u2bheavenbound, "Saddleback Church," 17:33.

We live in a post-secular age in the West that is spiritual, but wary of religion—especially Christianity. The Christian tradition in the West has been tried and found wanting. However, the democratic tradition and the Christian tradition have had a unique historical relationship. It looks different in each nation-state, but there has been a connection between Christianity and democracy. I have tried to show that the early theological metaphors for democracy in America were animated by monarchical and theocratic Israel, and that this metaphor was mistaken—there are no biblical promises to America for a land or a blessing like there were to Ancient Israel. This mistaken metaphor created undue harm to both natives of America and to Africans who were captured and sold as slaves to work in the "promised land." It also created an expectation that a certain type of Christian should sit in the privileged seat of political power to make sure the nation goes in the right direction. I argued that the proper metaphor for the church in America is like any church in any other nation-state: exile. A nostalgic pining for a different era developed as culture shifted away from general Christian "mores." There was an attempt at secularizing the public square in order to mute the deleterious effects of religious intolerance, oppression, and violence, and a hope that religion would eventually fade into the background of cultural consciousness in favor of reason, science, and secular democracy. But I tried to show that spirituality and religion are more resilient than the secularists thought. Further, the democratic tradition, by its nature, needs a complementary tradition, or it will collapse in on itself because it doesn't produce the kind of virtue in its citizens that it requires to continue. Those who argue that the democratic tradition can stand alone usually try to infuse it with religious overtones to give it more texture and meaning. They smuggle religious sentiment into a tradition that is not sentimental. So I asked the question, "Why try to use religious imagery and sentiment when we can actually tap into the rich resources of religious traditions—and in my case, the Christian tradition?" But I also contended that the relationship between Christianity and democracy is two-way. Christianity does not just complement democracy, but the democratic tradition has prophetically challenged the Christian tradition. Where moral progress has occurred is exactly at the blurring of the lines of separation of church and state. The amalgamation of religious language and democratic promise has created moral movement in the right direction. Now we must turn to what it might look like if the prophetic tension between Christianity and democracy is maintained and encouraged.

5

Prophetic Politics

I HAVE BEEN USING the word "prophetic" to describe the relationship between the democratic tradition and the Christian tradition in America. This word has religious overtones, and can conjure ideas of men or women warning everyone of impending doom. It can project images of lonely people who cannot get a hearing for their messages of repentance, return, or recovering faithfulness. In the Jewish tradition, Isaiah, Jeremiah, and Daniel come to mind, and in the Christian tradition there is this odd figure of John the Baptist—"a voice crying out in the wilderness" (John 1:23). I don't have in mind the idea of predicting the future, or even a single voice that rises above the noise of the public square to remind everyone that something is wrong. What I mean by prophetic is that conversations happen which press a tradition toward greater maturity and faithfulness through the notion of epistemological challenge. This usually happens at the edges or the borders—where one is consistently knocking up against those who remind us that there is an "other" to be considered. Borders and boundaries do not just separate one from another—they are a place of learning and growth. The prophetic relationship between democracy and Christianity is at the borders of each tradition. I have been arguing that, if we pay attention to the "blur" at the borders, this will produce a richer and stronger democracy, and the same is true for Christianity. The prophetic relationship does not just flow in one direction.

In this chapter, I want to try to articulate how this kind of relationship might shape the church's public posture as it negotiates its future in a post-secular society. Hunter provocatively said that the best social strategy in this current era would be for the church to be quiet for a season until we can sort out what a faithful relationship between Christian faith and democratic politics might look like.[1] Hunter's analysis of the church's influence (or lack of influence) on the larger culture is that Christians have baptized themselves into the way that the dominant culture uses power, and as a result has lost a winsome witness in the world—and here Hunter is primarily concerned with the Western world.[2] Hunter argues that it would be wrong to recapitulate the culture wars and re-strategize how to hold onto the remaining political power that the church has; instead his prescription for the church is to recover what he calls a "faithful presence," which would mean using its power in a different kind of way. Of course, defining what is "faithful" seems to be as fluid as trying to define love; faithfulness seems to morph with the ideologies that drive a community. One Christian community's faithfulness is another's compromise.

I have argued in previous chapters that an increasingly pluralistic public square has difficulty reconciling different visions of the good because it lacks a common moral framework and language to adjudicate between right and wrong. Hunter takes this further and maintains that, when there is a lack of moral consensus, the leadership, influencers, and activity in a culture begins to politicize—to turn toward politics and law and the instrumentality of the state to solve public problems: "law increases as cultural consensus decreases."[3] In response to this lack of social solidarity and its declining influence in culture, the church made a political turn that had disastrous consequences for its public perception and witness.

In 2008, David Gushee published his book *The Future of Faith in American Public Policy*.[4] Also in 2008, Shane Claiborne published *Jesus for President*.[5] In 2010, Hunter published *To Change the World*.[6] In 1972 John Howard Yoder published *The Politics of Jesus*, and in 1985 Stanley Hauerwas published *Against the Nations*.[7] Recently, there has been a spate of books on the church's relationship to the state. All of them are in some way working to negotiate what it means to be faithful to the Christian tradition and define its relationship to government differently. Here I want to focus on

1. Hunter, *To Change the World*, 186.
2. Ibid., 100.
3. Ibid., 102.
4. Gushee, *Future of Faith*.
5. Claiborne and Haw, *Jesus for President*.
6. Hunter, *To Change the World*.
7. Yoder, *Politics of Jesus*; Hauerwas, *Against the Nations*.

the three main strategies that contributed to the politicizaton of the public conversation: the evangelical right, the evangelical left, and the evangelical center. All three strategies have important things to say about substantive moral questions, but all three put their hope on the political side of the ledger as the means to achieve those moral ends. The religious right seemed to be the first of the theologically conservative Christian groups out of the gate to fill the religious vacuum as the progressive church lost its distinctiveness from culture.

The genesis of the religious right can be traced back to the Fundamentalist/Modernist controversy. Conservative Christianity distinguished itself from a more liberal or progressive Christianity by asserting the authority of Scripture, the ubiquity of personal sin, and the necessity of personal conversion. Hunter argues that the right's social strategy for "changing the world" was to aggregate an increasing number of people who were converted to the Christian worldview, and then society would change; if you increase the number of people who are displaying Christian virtue, the virtue of a culture would rise along with it—a rising tide lifts all boats. Thus, cultural change was supposed to rise proportionally with the increased individual change that comes along with Christian moral formation.[8] Progressive Christianity possessed most of the cultural influence during that time, and many conservatives felt relegated to the margins of public thought because of their views of the Bible and its interpretation. *Time* Magazine put Reinhold Niebuhr on its cover as one of the most influential theologians in America in 1948 at the peak of the liberal Christian influence. Steven Miller has written about the twilight of liberal Christianity in the 1960s; he maintains that, during the cultural revolution, liberal Christianity had accommodated itself to culture in such a way that it was hardly distinguishable from the secular left. This created a religious and cultural gap that the Conservatives were happy to fill.

I've talked some about the postmodern turn after World War II, but something must be said about the cultural parentheses of the 1950s. Following World War II, America attempted to settle back into the rhythms it was most comfortable with before the adjustments that had to be made during wartime efforts, including re-capturing the centrality of the nuclear family. During times of war, everyone makes exceptions to further the cause and contribute to the war effort. During World War II, women took industrial and manufacturing jobs as the men were occupied with military service,

8. Hunter, *To Change the World*.

people migrated to the cities because this is where the jobs were, and family life began to shift to accommodate these changes. Families began to look different. However, when things settled it was difficult to return to those same rhythms. "Leave it to Beaver" was a popular television program that idealized the nuclear family as a stabilizing force in culture. But what was portrayed in that program was being betrayed in the transitions back to reality. New possibilities were opening up for women in the workplace as they demonstrated competence in roles that had been traditionally male-dominated. Some men who served in the military were having a difficult time finding their places again as they re-entered the workforce and the family, and we now know that the reality of post-traumatic stress disorder had an impact on how they related to work and their families. And the stories that came out of the war, especially the atrocities of the Holocaust, incited reflection—especially in the American academy—on the possibilities of the Modern Project moving forward: How could the Great Depression and two world wars happen if humanity was on a steady path of progress? How could the advancements of science produce a military weapon like the atomic bomb and the United States use it on Japanese civilians? How could the horrors of the Holocaust happen in an enlightened and industrialized West? This was a unique time because there was a settling (an attempt to return back to the normal rhythms of American life) and an unsettling (the escalation of putting modern assumptions under the microscope of scrutiny).

At the same time, a politically and theologically conservative movement was happening nationally. In the aftermath of World War II, the Cold War began. The Soviet Union, the only super power apart from the United States, was threatening to sweep up the carnage of World War II into communist ideology. The contrast between the Soviet Union (communist, socialist, Marxist, and atheist) and the United States (democratic, capitalist, and "Christian") enlivened conservative Christians and re-capitulated the impulse toward describing America as a "Christian nation." The stark contrast between the two military, cultural, and ideological superpowers and the relative ease with which the liberal Christian tradition identified with the secular left created an opening for the re-emergence of Christian conservatism to advance a moral agenda that might return America to its "Godly Heritage." It was in this period that "under God" was written into the Pledge of Allegiance and "In God We Trust" was added to American currency (1954 and 1956 respectively). And it was also during this time that the American democratic experiment was being hounded on all sides to begin to fulfill its promises for a wider swath of people.

Michael Walzer argues that this kind of religious counterrevolution—a return to orthodox beliefs and practices—should be expected in secular democracies. It just took longer to be realized in the uniqueness of American politics. Walzer argues that democracy in America, unlike its European counterparts, was not instituted through an upheaval of an already-established governing system. Rather, the early founders saw relative freedom for creating something in this "new land." He contends that the notion of a secular democracy was a tidy fit with the freedom of religion that the early founders established: "Pluralism pressed American Protestants toward toleration, disestablishment, and separation."[9] He maintains that, unlike other democratic revolutions, the nascent stages of the American experiment largely left the "women question" and the "race question" at the margins. But as American democracy grew into its post-World War II form, these questions would be thrust into the national conversation. This confluence of a renewed religious sensibility that contrasted with the atheism of the Soviet Union and the lack of anything characteristically different between the liberal Christian tradition (which had carried the public voice of the Christian tradition in the early twentieth century) and the secular left created a void for religious conservatism—especially evangelicals—to fill. And much like the Constantinian ethos of a Christian Roman Empire, the future of the gospel was tied to the future of America. Therefore, when the "race question," the "women question," the "gay question," and the "religious minority" question surfaced as the cultural application of academic flirtations with postmodernity, a conflict arose. The arguments to make space for other cultural narratives challenged the idea of a nationalistic Christianity (and the dual notions that America was uniquely tied to the progress of the gospel internationally and that America would be blessed if it returned to its gospel roots). As the cultural revolution gained momentum in the public conversation, in the academic institutions, and in the courts, the Culture Wars were set in motion.

Hunter and Gushee both chronicle the rise of the religious right in response to this cultural transformation.[10] The right's story goes like this: America was founded as a Christian nation; there is a direct line of reasoning from biblical mandate to public policy recommendations; something

9. Walzer, *Paradox of Liberation*, 138.
10. Gushee, *Future of Faith*.

has gone quite wrong and the future of America is at stake; the spiritual legacy of America has been stripped away by the secularists, especially the Supreme Court; Christians have been pushed to the margins of culture, particularly high culture, where secular elites control the conversation; the judgment of God is looming if we do not return to our roots; politics was the path that led to this impending judgment; the political is the way to return to God's good graces; and if we put Christians in power and appoint the right judges, then America will flourish once again under God's blessing. The first real attempt to recapture the culture was the effort to elect Jimmy Carter in the 1976 election. Carter was a born-again, Sunday-School teaching, Southern Baptist candidate—a perfect match for their early political hopes. In their subsequent disappointment with Carter's presidency, the religious right galvanized their resolve and went "all-in" with the Republican Party and Ronald Reagan. The Republican Party's pro-life, small-government, strong-defense, and faith-and-family platform resonated with those on the right who were displaced from the mainstream of cultural conversation and cynical about the future of America. At its best, the religious right was constituted of well-meaning citizens with a hope to make the world a better place. But their use of culture-war rhetoric and their demands for a nostalgic return to the past all signaled their "loss, disappointment, anger, antipathy, resentment and desire for conquest."[11] Hunter concludes that "the Christian Right has generated greater hostility toward the Christian faith than ever before in the nation's history."[12] These are the motivating factors that contribute to his assertion that "Christians should remain silent for a season." This convolution of nationalism, political power, and a nostalgic view of Christian faith has muddled the meaning of the Christian faith being a "faithful presence" in the world.

Gushee argues that the evangelical left was awakened by the rhetoric of the religious right and the publicity that they were receiving. In contrast to the right's three core issues—abortion, homosexuality, and religious freedom (see the "Manhattan Declaration")[13]—and their keeping close company with Republicans, the evangelical left aligned themselves with the Democratic Party. Gushee argues that the evangelical left's core concerns were war, race, and economic justice. Angry at the perceived influence that the religious right had and the attention they were getting by the media, the

11. Hunter, *To Change the World*, 131.

12. Ibid., 125.

13. "Manhattan Declaration," http://manhattandeclaration.org/index.html.

evangelical left wanted to make sure that another Christian voice was heard in the political conversation. Jim Wallis's *New York Times* best-selling book *God's Politics* reflected a desire for a different perspective on politics, and its message resonated with a cross-section of evangelicals who were disaffected by the religious right. Gushee argues that the same sense of entitlement and anger that characterized the right characterized the evangelical left as well (it was just directed at the right and not at the secularists). Both the religious right and the evangelical left instrumentalized the Hebrew Scriptures to fit their purposes and conflated America with ancient Israel: the right focused on the law and personal responsibility and the left focused on the prophets and justice.

After his criticism of both the evangelical left and right, Gushee goes on to argue for a third way to approach politics: an evangelical center. Not wanting to be limited to the right's narrow agenda and unquestioned alliance to the Republican Party, and the left's similarly narrow scope and pact with the Democratic Party, Gushee argues for a broader agenda that includes all of the issues of the right and the left, and an independence from party affiliation. He states, "We need a biblically grounded rethinking of Christianity's entire engagement with American culture. I offer here at least a rethinking of our engagement with American public policy."[14] The evangelical center wants to keep an adjusted platform of faith and family and include egality, equality, and justice—especially for the marginalized.[15] It also wants to maintain a more holistic and consistent Christian ethic in public policy conversations.

Hunter wants to add a fourth response in this religio/political milieu: the Anabaptists. For Hunter, the Anabaptists (he uses John H. Yoder and Stanley Hauerwas as the acolytes for this view) maintain a strong contrast between the church and the world. As I argued in chapter 4, Hauerwas's early work and even the titles of his books reflect this contrast. Hunter maintains that Yoder kickstarted the mainstream effort to argue for an Anabaptist perspective on public policy with his groundbreaking book *The Politics of Jesus*. In this book, Yoder makes the case that the church is a distinct social institution that does not live by the world's standards. Hunter states, "Where the identity of the Christian Right is forged largely through their opposition to secularism and secularists, where the identity of the Christian Left derives from their opposition to the Right, the collective

---

14. Gushee, *Future of Faith*, xv.
15. Sider and Knippers, *Toward an Evangelical Public Policy*.

identity of the neo-Anabaptists comes through their dissent from the State and the larger political economy and culture of late modernity."[16]

Hunter criticizes this view in three ways: (1) it recapitulates the sentiments of anger and disappointment that is found in all Christian responses to the political; (2) it naively has an over-realized ecclesiology—it puts too much faith in the community of faith; and (3) Anabaptist identity is actually a negation of culture—who they are depends on the state and what direction the state takes.

I think that Hunter has overstated these criticisms of the Anabaptists and has failed to put their arguments in the appropriate context. Similar to what Hunter is doing with his book, Yoder and Hauerwas were correcting what they thought was a misdirection of the church. And much like H. Richard Niebuhr, Hunter has created a caricature of Anabaptists as an easy foil in the negotiations between the church and culture. Many Anabaptists (and Yoder and Hauerwas themselves) went beyond their early work to develop a more nuanced view of the church's relationship to the culture in their subsequent writings. This is the difficulty in articulating what it means to be a "faithful presence" because faithfulness is culturally conditioned. To have a faithful presence in Moscow during the height of Soviet Communism was different than having a faithful presence during the South Korean spiritual revivals in the early twentieth century.

Each of these four responses that Gushee and Hunter have outlined have some aspects of the prophetic nature of the relationship between Christianity and democracy, but like most responses to a different tradition, they have their extreme edges that need to be corrected; and we can take the positive (avoiding the extremes) to begin to form a prophetic politic (for the Christian tradition) for a post-secular age. The Anabaptists want to correct the notion that the church and the state go together. To be sure, there have been many positives of Christendom—too many to recount here (see Rodney Stark, *The Triumph of Christianity*, and John Ortberg, *Who is this Man?*, for accounts of how the Jesus movement was a positive force in Western culture).[17] In his seminal work, *The Politics of Jesus*, John Yoder argues that the church "is a visible socio-political, economic restructuring of relations among the people of God, achieved by divine intervention in the person of Jesus as the one Anointed and endued with the Spirit. Anchored in Isaiah 61—the blind see, the captives will be set free, the lame

---

16. Hunter, *To Change the World*.

17. Stark, *The Triumph of Christianity*; Ortberg, *Who Is This Man?*

walk."[18] For Yoder and many of the neo-Anabaptists, Jesus is the founder of a new social reality that presents an alternative (and thus a challenge) to the structures of the world. In contrast to Hunter's caricature (and Niebuhr's before him), this community is not marked by withdrawal from the world, but "a nonconformed quality of involvement in the world." Yoder sums up his view of this new sociopolitical reality in the world by saying,

> Jesus was not just a moralist whose teachings had some political implications; he was not primarily a teacher of spirituality whose public ministry unfortunately was seen in a political light; he was not just a sacrificial lamb preparing for his immolation, or a God-Man whose divine status calls us to disregard his humanity. Jesus was, in his divinely mandate (i.e., promised, anointed, messianic) prophethood, priesthood, and kingship, the bearer of a new possibility of human, social, and therefore political relationships.[19]

For Yoder, the first and foremost prophetic role that the church can take is to recover its authenticity as a tradition by being faithful to Jesus in its cultural context. Ironically, this is the argument that Hunter makes in his solution to how the church should relate to culture. He argues for a "faithful presence." This faithful presence is a dialectic of affirmation and antithesis—a relationship with the world that affirms that which God affirms and speaks out compassionately when the world goes against what God affirms.[20] As I argued in chapter 2, Jeremiah 29:1–7 plays an important role for both Yoder and Hunter in how the church can remain faithful to Jesus and still be "for the world."

It is important to emphasize that, in the first step in prophetic politics, for the church to be a faithful presence—or a new social reality with Jesus at its center—it must renegotiate its relationship to the state. There has to be some distinguishing characteristics that mark it out as something conspicuous from the state. This "distinguishing" requires two separate but concurrent efforts. All distinguishing is done in a cultural context and to argue that a religious tradition is outside of culture because it has a universal standard in its Ancient Scriptures, is to misunderstand revelatory religion. By God's very nature, the moment that God creates, God is bound to reveal what the world is like and what God is like in cultural idioms. To do something completely outside of those idioms would not be a revelation after all,

18. Yoder, *Politics of Jesus*, 32.

19. Ibid., 52.

20. Hunter, *To Change the World*, 281.

because people would have no context for understanding what God was doing. This creates a challenge for those in the cultural climate with immediate proximity to what is revealed (for example, the revelation of the gospels during Second Temple Judaism) and it is doubly a challenge for those whose framework has been formed with different cultural assumptions. This is obvious in the metaphors that the writers of Scripture use to describe God's work in the world. In first-century Palestine, the metaphors that are used in the pages of the gospels are generally agrarian: shepherds, farming, ranching, etc. When faith in Jesus spreads into the Roman Empire and the broader Gentile world, the writers of the Scripture use military and athletic metaphors (see Ephesians 6 and Hebrews 12 respectively). The writers of the New Testament outline a few practices that are central to the Christian tradition: the Eucharist, baptism, and gathering together for mutual encouragement and worship, prayer, and scripture study. As Christians we must distinguish what is authentically Christian in belief and practice, and how to practice this authenticity in our particular context. In other words, the first act of distinguishing what the church needs to do in prophetic politics is to discern what it means to be faithful to Jesus (what is an authentic Christian expression in our current cultural context).

The second act of distinguishing is in understanding the culture. If the church is going to live faithfully, following Jesus in any given cultural context, then it must understand both the Christian tradition and the culture they are rooted in. For example, the Apostle Paul articulated the gospel in Athens by appealing to their curiosity and their imperfect knowledge of the divine by attaching Jesus to their idea of an "unknown God." So he understood Athenian culture and was able to articulate the meaning of Jesus and his teachings in that context. But he didn't leave it there. For Paul, to be faithful to Jesus was not to place Jesus among the pantheon of Greco-Roman gods, but to distinguish God from their idols and mythology—God is not something made or represented by human hands (Acts 17:16–34). So we start with the church and its identity. Like all identities, it is understood as it relates to an "other," in this case, the world. Our questions about the Christian tradition and what it means to be faithful to Jesus are put in the light of what we are not (antithesis) and what we can affirm (affirmation) of the other.

The identity of the church as followers of Jesus is mediated through the Hebrew and Christian Scriptures. As the authoritative text of the Christian tradition, Scripture plays a central role in defining the authenticity of

Christian faith. For Protestants, Scripture is the sole arbiter of authority— the plumb line by which all other authorities are measured. The Catholic Christian tradition shares Scripture as an authority, but equally weights that authority with ecclesial authority and with church tradition. A variety of Christian traditions keep Scripture as authoritative for life and faith, but one of the unique challenges for Protestant Christians is the twofold doctrine of the priesthood of all believers and of sola scriptura (Scripture alone), and how that affects interpretation. These two doctrines put the interpretation of Scripture into the hands of congregants and shaves off the distinction between the trained clergy and "normal" parishioners. This democratizes interpretation and has fostered the wide varieties of denominations in the Protestant tradition. I've argued in chapter 2 that the Puritans got their interpretation wrong about equating America with theocratic Israel. I also touched on the social consequences of both sides of the Civil War using the Bible to justify their position on slavery. Getting our interpretation right is more difficult than Christians often make it out to be.

If we skip a rock across the lake that is the history of church, we will notice several places where some interpretations have proven false. The geocentric universe before Galileo's time is one of the more famous. I have used MacIntyre's definition to demonstrate how a tradition develops through its epistemological challenges to become thicker and more robust. This is a natural part of a tradition moving forward, and we should not be surprised if we have gotten something wrong in the past (actually, it should cause suspicion if a tradition does not have a set of beliefs that were once held that have now been shown to be false over time). But this raises a question of how to buffer the Christian tradition from unnecessarily holding false beliefs in their interpretation of their sacred texts. The goal of rational inquiry within any tradition is to maximize the number of true beliefs (those beliefs that fulfill our expectations about reality) and minimize the number of false beliefs (those that seem to always be contrary to reality).

One of the ways to avoid misinterpretation and the ethical consequences that come along with it is to borrow from the interpretive method of Judaism and apply it to Christianity. That is, move away from defending "doctrines of interpretation," like inerrancy, infallibility, etc., that try to hem in orthodoxy, and rather treat interpretation like a practice: we put our best interpretations into a community of interpreters and work out the meanings of the text in a particular cultural setting together. This does not mean that we give up on orthodoxy, but that orthodox interpretation has always been done within community. Christians do not need the mediating authority of a religious professional, but they do need to put their best interpretation into the community for conversation and discussion.

If we treat interpretation as a practice, then it has a set of virtues that distinguish it as a "good practice" that moves people toward the interpretive *telos*. I take the *telos* of the practice of interpretation as instructing people toward salvation and equipping followers of Jesus for "every good work":

> But as for you, continue in what you have learned and firmly believed, knowing from whom you learned it, and how from childhood you have known the sacred writings that are able to instruct you for salvation through faith in Christ Jesus. All scripture is inspired by God and is useful for teaching, for reproof, for correction, and for training in righteousness, so that everyone who belongs to God may be proficient, equipped for every good work. (2 Tim 3:14–16)

This passage outlines a fourfold path toward becoming proficient in our interpretive practice: (1) teaching (we learn something new from Scripture); (2) reproof (we learn our misdirection); (3) correction (we learn how to correct our misdirection); and (4) training in righteousness (Scripture teaches us how to bring ourselves under the teachings of God so that we might reflect God in the world).

While the writers of Scripture never systematically outline a set of virtues for the practice of interpretation, I think that we can discern at least five as we read the pages of the New Testament. I have put these in an order intentionally because I think that they flow more naturally and produce a better result if thought about in sequence, but they do not have to be kept in sequence. The first virtue of interpretation is hard work: "Do your best to present yourself to God as one approved by him, a worker [a person who works hard] who has no need to be ashamed, rightly explaining the word of truth" (2 Tim 2:15). This passage should be a caution for twenty-first-century readers and interpreters. The author of 2 Timothy is reminding his readers of the necessity of the work that it takes to understand and apply the life, death, resurrection, and teachings of Jesus in the context of Second Temple Judaism. Fast-forward two millennia, and it seems like the work that it takes to understand Jesus in the context of all the messianic hopes and expectations of Second Temple Judaism and apply that to our specific situation today takes a considerable amount of effort. The Hebrew and Christian Scriptures are a layered text with depths of meaning; it takes disciplined study to move beyond devotional inspiration to understanding its profundity for moral formation.

The second virtue is patience. There is a story in Acts 5 that illustrates this virtue. The Apostles are imprisoned by the religious rulers of the time and questioned before a council. These early followers of Jesus appealed to the authority of God in their public preaching and eschewed the religious leaders' warnings to stop. The response of the leaders was rage and a desire to kill them; but Gamaliel argued that they should be patient, to let the fruit of their ministry become evident so that they could test whether it was from God or not. The Christian community, especially evangelicals, are very quick to rush denouncements over what they think is "unorthodox." The idea of patience hedges against one's rush to judgment and interpretation through the lens of what comes most naturally to us.

The third virtue of interpretation is humility. After "faith, hope, and love," humility is the most-mentioned virtue in the Christian life. Proverbs 3, James 4, and 1 Peter 5 all state that "God opposes the proud, but gives grace to the humble." The author of Philippians argues for humility that is modeled after Christ—"who did not consider equality with God as something to be exploited, but emptied himself, taking the form of a slave" (Phil 2:6–7). Further, James cautions against wanting to become teachers because of the greater strictness with which teachers will be judged. The author goes on to say, "For all of us *make many mistakes*" (emphasis mine). Given Christian history (where those mistakes and their consequences are evident), given James's warning here: that we should be careful about positioning ourselves to be teachers, given that one of the core doctrines of the Christian tradition is depravity—that we bend the moral universe in our direction, and given that we human beings are finite in our knowledge, this bundle of cautions should create a sense of humility in rushing to validate our interpretation.

The fourth virtue is to put our best interpretations into a diverse community of interpreters. Those that do not always see the writings of Scripture through the same lens that you do can buffer your drift toward being affirmed by the affirming. How do we avoid this kind of confirmation bias when we only talk with those who disagree with us? Again, I have MacIntyre's notion of epistemological challenges in mind here. The idea is that an internal challenge will create a sort of tension that is different than external challenges. If your interpretation cannot stand up to close scrutiny by those who disagree with you, but hold the same basic convictions that you do; or if you are not willing to entertain any challenges to your best interpretation, your tradition is fundamentally weaker. This virtue of placing your interpretation into a diverse community of interpreters creates a buffer to our propensity to bend our best interpretations to fit into our particular lenses, and it opens possibilities that our finite minds might not have entertained. For example, serious debate and discussion continues in conservative Christian circles about the nature of the atoning work of Christ. Neo-Calvinists emphasize the penal-substitutionary work of Christ to satisfy God's wrath by punishing Christ for humanity's sins; others emphasize the *Christus Victor* work of Christ, or Christ redeeming all the world back to himself by defeating Satan and the dark forces in the world. The proponents of these two models of atonement (there are more than these two) are better when they put their best case forward in the other community, and this fourth virtue produces a better interpretation.[21]

Finally, the fifth virtue is to communicate your interpretive convictions with gentleness and respect. First Peter 3:15–17 says to "set apart Christ as Lord, always be ready to make your defense to anyone who demands from you an accounting for the hope that is in you; yet do it with gentleness and reverence [respect]." The author of 1 Peter is connecting this notion of communicating about faith to the fruits that the Spirit produces as a person grows in Christ. This echoes Paul's words in Galatians: "but the fruit of the Spirit is love, joy, peace, patience, kindness, generosity, faithfulness, gentleness, and self-control. There is no law against such things" (Gal 5:22–23). The notion here is to have an interpretive understanding that has moved through these virtues, becomes more settled as it encounters and responds to external and internal challenges, and is defended without being defensive. We are interpreting to learn and grow toward maturity in Christ, and that process is incomplete (no matter how much education we might have, or how long one has been a Christian).

What I have been trying to say is that the Hebrew and Christian Scriptures are central to defining the identity of followers of Jesus, the church, and that this is the first step in the distinguishing process. Hunter's instincts are right, and borrowed from the Anabaptists—the church must be the church in order to be a faithful presence in culture. Since the Scriptures are central, their interpretation is important, but the history of the church is littered with misinterpretation. To do its best, the church should

---

21. For an example of how this virtue can be applied, see Beilby and Eddy, *Nature of the Atonement.*

view the interpretation of Scripture as a practice—with a *telos* and a core set of virtues. The more skilled one becomes at this practice, the more developed its identity and ethic becomes—interpretation becomes thicker, richer, more substantive, and more authentic. Consequently, the church can become more discerning about the distinguishing marks between itself and the surrounding culture.

It is in this discernment that prophetic politics is central. Hunter defines culture as "an accumulation of values held by the majority of people and the choices made based on those values."[22] This includes both formal institutions, like government, and the informal institutions that make up civil society. In talking about distinguishing, it is important to understand the distinction between these two aspects of culture. The formal institutions have been encoded with certain qualities that are ideally accessible to all. We can look at the laws and processes and define the important characteristics and functions of formal institutions. The informal institutions and loose associations are a bit more difficult—they rely on an assumed background framework that may or may not be explicit. What I am most concerned with in this book is the church's relationship to the formal institutions of government, but the informal institutions play an important role as well.

As I stated in chapter 2, the New Testament is relatively ambiguous about what kind of government best represents God in the world. The nascent church was birthed inside two governments—the Jewish government nested (not comfortably) inside the Roman government. Jesus' trial and crucifixion brought this conflation of two governments into focus where the leaders of the Jewish community accuse Jesus before Roman leadership because only the Romans could carry out the death penalty. The New Testament does outline a way to relate to the world (culture): the government is an institution that is created good—a kind of common grace to provide for people's flourishing (Col 1:15–17) but it is also an institution that has been infected by and corrupted by the presence of sin in individuals and in the structures and institutions of societies—both formal and informal. This produces a natural tension that will result in antinomy between the church and the world: The community of faith is supposed to be in the world, but not of it (John 17). The way in which the community of followers of Jesus is supposed to be in the world is as "salt" and "light" (Matt 5:13–17); and the church's relationship to any culture is as aliens and exiles with dual

22. Hunter, *To Change the World*, 6.

citizenship (1 Pet 2:11–12; Phil 3:20; Eph 2:19–20), with primary allegiance to the Lordship of Christ and to the good of all people (1 Pet 3:13–17).

Dubbed as America's theologian, Reinhold Niebuhr argued that the corporate and social nature of sin is something that develops in institutions over time. For Niebuhr, it is important to understand how "group pride" (or group sin) emerges from the pride of individuals. While the individual is the moral agent, group pride develops a life of its own as it takes a qualitatively different tenet than the aggregation of individual pride. As a result, it can then take on a life of its own and "achieve a certain kind of authority over the individual and results in unconditioned demands by the group upon the individual."[23] Further, Niebuhr argues that the pretensions of group pride go beyond the pretensions of the individual: "the group is more arrogant, hypocritical, self-centered, and more ruthless in the pursuit of its ends than the individual."[24] This is why individuals will participate in the activities of a mob, but would never consider doing some of the same activities that the mob is doing when by themselves. For Niebuhr, group pride and egotism most often gets expressed in the formal institutions of a nation-state

> because the state gives the collective impulses of the nation such instruments of power and presents the imagination of individuals with such obvious symbols of its discrete collective identity that the national state is most able to make absolute claims for itself, to enforce those claims by power and to give them plausibility and credibility by the majesty and panoply of its apparatus . . . obedience is prompted by the fear of power on the one hand and by reverence for majesty on the other.[25]

For Niebuhr, the state conveys the authoritative and legislative expression of group will, while a "prophetic minority" is the instrument of the state's self-transcendence—its conscience.[26] This ability of the state to transcend individuals and amass an authority over individuals reflects the same impression of sin on the individual. The state has a tension of being created for the good of the people, but taking on a kind of quality that asserts its own pride and egotism.

---

23. Niebuhr, *Nature and Destiny of Man*, 208.
24. Ibid., 208.
25. Ibid., 209.
26. Ibid., 210.

Since the state no longer fully or perfectly mediates the flourishing of its citizens and can at times actively oppose God (Rom 8:38), those passages about submissive participation to the state in Romans 13 and 1 Peter 2 are accompanied by passages of prayer for leaders (1 Tim 2:1–4). I have written already about the dual role of government: to promote the good and to punish the evil—again a loosely defined role, but one with some background assumptions in the definitions of good and evil—that provide broad parameters for the charge to "submit." I take submission to mean at least three things: (1) to participate at the level that is available to you. This means different things in different contexts. For leaders, it means the just exercise of power for others; for citizens in a democracy, it means voting to the best of one's ability for those people and programs that will fulfill the governmental mandate to promote good and punish evil; and for members of the community who are non-citizens, it means a reorientation of how to participate while one may not have all the rights, privileges, and obligations of a full member of the community. (2) The second meaning of submission is in the church's role to prophetically affirm and partner with the powers and structures of government when they are "doing good." Like individuals, nation-states (powers and structures) are created for a good purpose and reflect the order and grace of God necessary for human flourishing. Where this is happening both in its positive affirmations (love), and its negations (justice), the church can wholeheartedly contribute to a state or locally sponsored initiative (even though the result might be less than ideal). For example, San Francisco's Unified School District has developed the Foster Youth Services Program (FYS) to help quell the disjointed education of many of the foster children in the city. FYS provides support for the educational needs of foster children, helps to educate the schools on the challenges that foster children face, and aids foster children's transition from high school to college. This is an obvious case when a governmental institution is doing good and the church can affirm and partner with the work that FYS is doing. (3) The third way that the church can participate in submission is to prophetically challenge and not participate with the powers and structures of government when they have flipped their God-ordained role and turn out to promote evil (injustice) instead of good. Martin Luther King Jr. played this prophetic role for blacks in America in the Civil Rights Movement, and later in his activism in protest of the Vietnam War. This non-participation is a way to fulfill the submission mandate and still maintain that the government is not fulfilling its role. When it comes to this third way, the church also submits to the authorities when it protests evil. Those who protest in this way recognize that their civil disobedience comes at a price—they will incur the wrath of the state—but they have counted the cost of that price and are willing to pay. Here is where we find the example of Dietrich Bonhoeffer. I have already mentioned Bonhoeffer's prescient resistance to the Nazis that eventually cost him his life. His participation in the Confessing Church and the resistance movement marked him as one who was opposing the powers and authorities of the Nazi government. His participation in the Valkyrie coup took that opposition to the extreme edges of submission. What people often overlook is that Bonhoeffer saw his own part in the resistance movement as being *for* Germany. He used his international contacts and expertise to help build a "shadow government" that was ready to step in should Valkyrie be successful.[27] He wanted Germany to be the best nation that it could be, and his resistance was a part of that desire.

I have outlined three ways to participate in government and contribute to the common good. These all assume some kind of voice and power in the political conversation. But what if this is missing? Democracies promote the individual voice and make space for secondary associations in civil society—the more secure democracies give their citizens the freedom of speech and the right to assemble—even when that speech is directed against the authorities and the assembly is promoting something that runs counter to the accepted "mores" of society. But there are times when those privileges are suspended, or Christians find themselves in other forms of government where those rights are not held. The church may still go through the processes outlined above—but what if followers of Christ are not allowed to participate? This was and sometimes still is the case in Communist or Islamic nations. My argument for voluntarily going into exile in America is quite different than those who are exiles in a hostile and unwelcome culture.

The New Testament writers used imagery of Israel in exile to describe the church. Here I want to take those images and expand on them. What does it mean to be in exile, and how are we supposed to live out our faith in a sometimes hostile culture? The stories of Joseph, Moses, Daniel, and Esther were meant to inspire the Israelites to stay faithful to Yahweh during difficult circumstances. In the words of Psalm 137:4, "How can we sing the songs of the Lord while in a foreign land?" I think that we can learn

27. Bethge, *Dietrich Bonhoeffer.*

something about what it means to sing that song as aliens and exiles in a foreign land from these stories.

Daniel Smith argues that the Jewish community developed a fourfold response to the threat of destruction by the Babylonians or the danger of assimilation into their society. First, they adopted a pattern of social organization, with tightly knit groups of people who had authority to provide leadership in maintaining their identity. Second, those leaders mediated between the exiled community and the host culture. They were the ones to negotiate what it was going to be like to live in that culture. Third, they developed stories, a folklore of heroic figures whose cleverness and courage saved the Jews from their enemies. Finally, they developed practices that set them apart from the dominant society. I want to focus on the third response: their stories and folklore of heroic figures.

Joseph, Moses, Daniel, and Esther are four of those figures.[28] Without recounting the details of all the stories (each deserves a book of its own) there are common threads that are apparent in all four. Each was a Hebrew, an Israelite, a Jew (those terms are used successively in history to refer to the descendants of Abraham) and each found themselves in a foreign land (Egypt, Babylon, and Persia respectively). They were tested in their commitment to Yahweh, Israel's God, and their stories were recorded as examples of what it means to be faithful to Yahweh in a difficult situation. Despite their unique circumstances, common themes run throughout their stories. We want to get at these themes to see if there is something to learn by analogy for our own time. Here are several that stand out.

These stories of exile are born out of adverse circumstances. Joseph was sold into slavery by his brothers; Moses was to be a victim of genocide until his mother risked his life (and hers) by placing him in a reed basket in the Nile River; and Daniel and Esther faced different circumstances—Jerusalem was devastated, the temple destroyed and they were taken from their homeland as captives of the Babylonian Empire (and then Persia). In each case, something negative started their story, but as the story develops, it turns constructive. In the long view, God uses these difficult circumstances to accomplish something good in the world. The second thread in these four stories is that each displayed a vocational excellence. They performed their assigned tasks in such a way that they stood out among their peers. They each became elites in one way or another in their host culture because of their unique abilities to fulfill the assigned roles given to them. This gave

28. Smith's argument is found in Friesen, *Artists, Citizens, Philosophers*.

them opportunities for advancement and influence in their respective cultures. The third common theme is that God gifted each one of them with a special gifting for their circumstance. For Joseph and Daniel, it was the interpretation of dreams. For Moses, it was to be the mouthpiece of God, and for Esther, it was the wisdom to know how to navigate the royal court of Persia. These unique gifts allowed them access to cultural leadership and gave them influence incommensurate to their social status as a foreigner. Fourth, God uses their natural gifts and abilities to accomplish his tasks: Joseph's administrative ability, Moses' proximity to Pharoah and his family, Daniel and Esther's wisdom and attractiveness. Each of these "natural" gifts and abilities contributed to their capability to have influence in their host culture. The fifth theme is that each of them faced a crisis of character. Will they compromise their faith in Yahweh for advantage or survival in this foreign and sometimes hostile environment? Each of them passes the test: Joseph resists the sexual advances of Potiphar's wife; Moses runs against his family and culture to rescue the Israelites; Daniel resists the directives to compromise kosher and prayer; and Esther, along with Mordecai, refused to worship another deity. They maintained faithfulness to God despite the pressures that were continually placed on them to compromise their faith. Sixth, each of them gained favor with the influential leaders of the particular host culture—they were people who were in the "courts of the King"; their access gave them opportunity to do things that others could not do. And finally, each contributed to the flourishing of the community: Joseph saves the ancient Near East from famine, Moses delivers the Israelites from slavery in Egypt, Daniel is the catalyst for Nebuchadnezzar's move toward Israel's God, and Esther rescues the Jewish community in Persia from genocide.

These stories suggest a starting place for the prophetic relationship with culture when it proscribes faith: to develop practices that mark the community of faith as distinct and to understand the cultural context. This clarifies the discernment process of what makes up compromise and what does not. There is an important detail in the story of Daniel that is an anecdote of discernment. Notice that Daniel renegotiated the food offered to them because the Babylonian cuisine surely violated kosher, but he did nothing about the Babylonian process of "renaming" that changed their Hebrew names to reflect Babylonian deities; he did, however, refuse the king's edict to bow to the idolatrous statue and pray to Yahweh instead of Nebuchadnezzar. This is a nuanced and subtle response to different aspects of culture that threatened to compromise their faith. There was creativity in renegotiating the king's food, there was submission in their renaming, and there was resistance in prayer. Further, notice how the author of Hebrews describes Moses: he "chose to be identified with the people of God" and suffered as a result (Heb 11:24–25). He gave up the power and privilege of Pharaoh's family for the sake of following God. It goes on to say that they had a long view of faithfulness: "Yet all these, though they were commended for their faith, did not receive what was promised" (Heb 11:39). The idea of being faithful to God may not have an immediate external reward, or any reward at all. It is a part of what it means to be a follower of Jesus, and therefore is intrinsically rewarding.

In these stories, there is more to a prophetic relationship with culture than just survival. Here we return to Jeremiah. I have tried to create the theological architecture to understand that the church in the world is analogous to Israel in exile. This creates space to borrow metaphors from Judaism in analogous cases where they are working out their faith away from the land, the temple, and the practices that were so central to their religious and cultural life. That was the question that Jeremiah was trying to answer for those taken to Babylon, who were asking what to do now: "Build houses and live in them; plant gardens and eat what they produce. Take wives and have sons and daughters; take wives for your sons, and give your daughters in marriage; multiply there and do not decrease. But seek the welfare of the city where I have sent you into exile, and pray to the Lord on its behalf, for in its welfare you will find your welfare" (Jer 29:5–7). The author of Jeremiah is encouraging the Jewish community to flourish in Babylon—to seek *shalom* for all people as they waited and worked toward their return. This sentiment is echoed in relationship to the communities that were forming around Jesus in 1 Peter: "Now who will harm you if you are eager to do what is good? But even if you do suffer for doing what is right, you are blessed . . . For it is better to suffer for doing good, if suffering should be God's will, than to suffer for doing evil. For Christ also suffered for sins once for all, the righteous for the unrighteous, in order to bring you to God" (1 Pet 3:13–18).

This word for "good" used in 1 Peter 3:13–18, *agathos*, is in the family of words that are used in Romans 13 and 1 Peter 2 to describe the government's role as an institution in the world. It has connotations of doing something beneficial, honorable and morally right.[29] It is a general word that

29. Vine et al., *Vine's Complete Expository Dictionary*.

assumes a shared moral language—everyone should be able to recognize when good is happening. In Jeremiah's language, it is to be "for the city" and the welfare of another. *Agathos* is used 102 times in the New Testament, and is often contrasted with evil. For example, Romans 12:9 says, "hate what is evil, hold fast to what is good." It is a consistent reminder that the community that follows Christ is to follow the Golden Rule—to love God and love our neighbors as ourselves (Matt 22:34–40). "Doing good" is the tangible expression of this love.

In chapter 3, I argued that this is a supererogatory virtue that moves beyond the democratic virtues of "do no harm" and is done without reservation or condition. To do "good" is the Christian response to both blessing and suffering (Rom 12:14). It brings the friend, the neighbor, and the "enemy" into moral view. Again, the writers of the New Testament model their notion of good on Jesus Christ. In 1 Peter 3, the admonition to do good is followed by the example of Christ "suffering for the unrighteous." In Romans 5, Christ's death and reconciling work on the cross is connected to his love for those who are his enemies (vv. 8–10).

The church's prophetic relationship to culture is one of faithfulness to the teachings of Christ expressed in the broad Christian tradition. It takes discernment in how to live out that faithfulness in a particular cultural context, participating in the governing processes according to the appropriate laws and systems. This means that the church can affirm and partner with institutions of a culture (whether formal or voluntary) when those institutions are fulfilling their mandate: promoting the good of each citizen and punishing evil. It also means speaking and nonviolently acting against the institutions of a culture that have flipped its mandate: they promote evil and punish good. This may come with consequences that result in suffering, mistreatment and possible persecution. There are no conditions in the New Testament that preclude this kind of "being for the city" if one is experiencing those negative consequences. The church is to always be doing good for others, no matter the circumstances.

Finally, the last prophetic role that the church plays in culture is to be a model community that proclaims Jesus as Lord and demonstrates the wisdom of God. I will borrow a metaphor here from the Hebrew Scriptures that is reaffirmed in the New Testament. In Deuteronomy, the author recapitulates the Law and its purposes in Israel's cultic, moral, and political life:

> See, just as the LORD my God has charged me, I now teach you
> statutes and ordinances for you to observe in the land that you are

about to enter and occupy. You must observe them diligently, for this will show your wisdom and discernment to the peoples who, when they hear all these statutes, will say, "Surely this great nation is a wise and discerning people!" For what other great nation has a god so near to it as the LORD our God is whenever we call to him? And what other great nation has statutes and ordinances as just as this entire law that I am setting before you today? (Deut 4:5–8)

Because the church is not a nation, but an international community within nations, it does not have political commands as Israel did, so we must "climb the ladder of abstraction" in order to find points where a one-to-one analogy is warranted and appropriate application can be drawn. In this case, Israel is the community of faith that follows Yahweh as Lord. They are to live out the commands of God—the Law—to demonstrate God's wisdom, nearness, and benevolence to the surrounding nations. The church is analogous to this in that it is a community of faith that follows Jesus as Lord and demonstrates the wisdom, nearness, and benevolence of God to onlookers from within each nation. Matthew 5:13–16 seems to reiterate this expression of purpose:

> You are the salt of the earth; but if salt has lost its taste, how can its saltiness be restored? It is no longer good for anything, but is thrown out and trampled under foot. You are the light of the world. A city built on a hill cannot be hid. No one after lighting a lamp puts it under the bushel basket, but on the lampstand, and it gives light to all in the house. In the same way, let your light shine before others, so that they may see your good works and give glory to your Father in heaven.

Here, Jesus is making this same analogy by using the imagery of Jerusalem—the center-city of Israel—as a city on a hill whose light shines outward. The community of faith that calls Jesus Lord is to be that city—one that sheds light into the world. This notion of light is carried throughout the New Testament to depict the work of Jesus and the good that those who might follow him will do in the world. The writer of John begins his Gospel with "In the beginning . . . All things came to being through him [Christ]. What has come into being in him was life, and the life was the light of all people. The light shines in the darkness and the darkness did not overcome it" (John 1:1–5). Christian morality—which is primarily for the community of faith that calls Jesus Lord—can run counter to the currents of popular culture and the legislative work of the formal governmental institutions.

When this countercultural moral stream exacerbates public conflict in the democratic sphere there are really two options: (1) to galvanize all the power that is possible in order to legislate a specific moral agenda (the strategy of the religious right), or (2) to demonstrate the wisdom of that moral agenda in their community. I have affirmed Hunter's contention that the Nietzschean political strategy of number 1 has actually obscured the good news of the gospel, so I think that number 2 is the right alternative. As with Ancient Israel, legislation that was designed and aimed at the "people of God" was to be adopted, not legislated for those outside of that community. This is true with the community of faith that calls Jesus Lord—Christian morality is supposed to be adopted but not legislated, convincing but not coercive. As I mentioned in chapter 2, Walzer's notion of the church's role in society recovers this idea of modeling over legislating. Here is the fuller quotation of Walzer's conclusion:

> One day, however, that security becomes a habit and zeal is no longer a worldly necessity [speaking of the revolutions]. Then the time of God's people is over. In this world, the last word always belongs to the worldlings and not to the saints. It is a complacent word and it comes when salvation, in all its meanings, is no longer a problem. *But the saints have what is more interesting: the first word. They set the stage of history for the new order.*[30]

Religious zeal is necessary if it is focused on the right things. The final chapter is about those right things. What does it mean to be first-word Christians?

---

30. Walzer, *Revolution of the Saints*, 319. Emphasis mine.

6

Experiments in Exile

WHAT DOES IT MEAN to "set the stage of history?" If I can recapture my argument in the introduction: we live in a post-secular age—this is a transitional epoch that has several defining characteristics: people are spiritual, are looking for something to tie their experiences together with a bigger narrative—but not the kind of metanarrative that was defined by the powerful and was oppressive during the Modern Era, and they are okay with some mystery in their life. They are wary of religious traditions, especially in the public square, because religious absolutism runs counter to the compromise necessary for a plurality of people to live together peacefully. They are also wary of religion because, historically, violence has been done in the name of religion. Even if that violence is done at the extreme edges of a particular religion, the possibility remains that religion produces this kind of thing. But the majority of people still hold out hope that religion can contribute to solving some of our most pressing social problems. My argument is that these trends indicate that the people who are familiar with the Christian tradition, even if they do not identify themselves within that tradition, want Christianity to recover its first-word impulse and promote the flourishing of the community. At a fundamental level, this is what they understand as authentic religious expression. Like the author of the book of James suggests, "Religion that is pure and undefiled before God, the Father, is this: to care for orphans and widows in their distress, and to keep oneself unstained by the world" (Jas 1:27). There is also a suspicion that the way in which Christians (especially evangelicals) have participated in politics has unnecessarily stained the church.

In the Hebrew Scriptures, the idea of human flourishing is captured in the word *shalom:* a kind of wholeness and wellbeing that is connected to relational peace. *Shalom* is often translated "peace." In the New Testament, this idea is carried forward in the word *life*. The author of the gospel of John records the association between the work of Christ and *shalom/life* in this way: "Now Jesus did many other signs in the presence of his disciples, which are not written in this book. But these are written so that you may come to believe that Jesus is the Messiah, the Son of God, and that through believing you may have life in his name" (John 20:30–31). This is the goal: life.

Dallas Willard has argued that evangelicals have distorted this idea of "life" to mean exclusively "eternal life," or heaven. He maintains that belief in Christ is not the ending point of following Jesus, but the starting point for a distinctive kind of life that begins now.[1] This life is characterized by the good works of the church and specific virtues that mark out followers of Christ (Galatians 5:22–23). If we take the author of the Gospel of John's view and set it in Willard's context—that evangelicals have often emphasized belief in Christ as the ending point and not the starting point—we can begin to develop what an "eternal kind of life" looks like. And this can be helpful to the evangelical church in recovering its prophetic role in the politics of a pluralistic culture.

The author of John uses the word for "life" and its iterations approximately thirty-five times in his Gospel, the most of any New Testament writer.[2] If we work backward from the purpose statement in John 20:30–31 to the first few verses in John 1:1–5 it is quite clear that the author is setting the kind of life that Jesus offers into the background framework of the first few chapters of Genesis: "in the beginning" is a distinct echo of Genesis 1:1. And whether you take the genre of Genesis to be mythology, historical narrative, or some kind of poetic reality, it is clear that the author of John is positioning the ministry of Jesus in the setting of the creation story of the Hebrew Bible. Other echoes abound in the first few verses of John as well: "all things came into being through him," "life," "light," and "darkness" are all themes found in the first few chapters of Genesis and the first few verses of John. There is a clear sense of the author's use of the Hebrew creation story to set the stage for Jesus and to denote the continuity between the

---

1. Willard, *Divine Conspiracy*, 14.
2. Wigram and Winter, *Word Study Concordance*, 339.

Jewish expectation of *shalom* in God's plan and the life offered in the redemptive work of Jesus Christ.

Without going into a full exegetical treatment of the first few chapters of Genesis, I want to try to make this connection between *shalom* and life and its implications for my argument in this book. The *Jewish Study Bible* describes how to approach the interpretation of Genesis in this way:

> The book of Genesis is thus, in more sense than one, a primary source for Jewish theology. It presents its ideas on the relationship of God to nature, to the human race in general, and to the people Israel in particular in ways that are, however, foreign to the expectations of most modern readers. It is therefore all too easy to miss the seriousness and profundity of its messages. For the vehicle through which Genesis conveys its worldview is neither the theological tract nor the rigorous philosophical proof nor the confession of faith. That vehicle is, rather, narrative.[3]

In the first pages of Genesis, we have a depiction of both what the kingdom of God might look like in its idyllic state (Gen 1–2) and the devastating consequences that human sin had on that kingdom (Gen 3).[4] I've used Reinhold Niebuhr's notion of corporate sin—sin embedded in the institutions and structures of the world—and the traditional evangelical understanding of personal sin as essential to the Christian tradition. But this idea is inherited from the Jewish tradition. From Genesis chapter 3 onward, the Hebrew Bible is concerned with the redemptive work of God in addressing the problem of sin and its consequences. When the New Testament was written, there was a strong expectation that a coming messianic figure would deliver them from the oppression of the Roman Empire (i.e., deliver them from exile) into an idyllic theocratic nation-state. These expectations were grounded in their historical narrative that had its foundations in their creation stories. And the Apostle Paul connects this expectation with the person and redemptive work of Jesus. He says that "at just the right time" in this historical narrative, Jesus did something unique (Rom 5:6). Bruce Waltke and Cathi Fredricks summarize the connection between the life and teachings of Jesus and the first pages of Israelite history in Genesis in this way: "Jesus Christ's offer of the kingdom of God in the Synoptic Gospels brings the expectation of the Primary History that God will establish his

3. Berlin et al., *Jewish Study Bible*, 8.

4. For a fuller treatment of this, see Futato, "Because It Had Rained"; Walton, *The Lost World of Genesis One*.

moral kingdom over the nations through national Israel to its fulfillment."[5] The first chapters of Genesis are *"historical, ideological, and aesthetic . . . it is ideological art."*[6]

The focal point of the picture of *life* and *shalom* in Genesis is the intimate and benevolent relationship between Yahweh and humanity. This is seen in God's act of breathing into humanity the breath of life (Gen 2:7) and the conversational nature of the relationship between the first couple and God (Gen 3:8–10). Much has been said about the nature of this relationship—its idyllic state in chapters 1 and 2, and the alienation in chapter 3—and in many evangelical circles the conversation about Jesus and the abundant life stops here. Jesus' redemptive work on the cross means a reconciliation of the alienation from God that happened as a result of sin and an ultimate restoration of the idyllic state of Eden in heaven; rather than ending, the story begins in Genesis and in Jesus' ministry. An abundant life spins outward from the hub of an intimate relationship with God to affect all other areas of life.

There are five core relationships in Genesis chapters 2 and 3 that are created good and corrupted or fractured by the presence of sin. We have already talked about the primary relationship: between God and humanity. The second important relationship is between humanity and the environment. God places human beings in a garden (Gen 2:8), and this garden is filled with lavish provision of food, water and beauty—all that humanity needed for their flourishing and more. The description of this garden contains many of the pleasing and precious things known to the ancient world, like gold, bdellium, and lapis lazuli (Gen 2:12). This emphasis on the environment continues throughout Genesis, such as when God promises to give Abraham a land and covenantal laws were established to protect the land (the Sabbatical year, Exodus 23:10–11) and to re-appropriate the land (the Year of Jubilee, Leviticus 25) so that everyone had a place and economic opportunity. While the land does not play a prominent role in the life of the church (see my description in chapter 2), the Apostle Paul does speak of how the environment and humanity are uniquely tied together as "creation longs for the revealing of the people of God" (Rom 8:19–22). In Genesis chapter 3, alienation occurs between humanity and its environment as Adam and Eve are removed from the garden and placed into the wilderness (Gen 3:24–25).

5. Waltke and Fredricks, *Genesis*, 54.
6. Ibid., 31.

The third relationship essential to an abundant life found in Genesis is humanity's relationship with work. God placed human beings into the garden "to till it and tend it" (2:15). The lush vegetation that was produced needed to be cared for, and it was humanity's job to manage it—to work it. They were supposed to be stewards over all that God had created. As is the case in each of the five relationships, humanity's relationship with work suffers the same consequences of sin as its relationship with God and the environment: alienation occurs that makes work difficult. Thorns and thistles grow and it will now take "the sweat of your brow" to produce what is necessary to live (Gen 3:17–18).

Again, the author of the Pentateuch addresses this particular relationship by establishing a rhythm of work and rest in the laws concerning the Sabbath (Deut 5:12–15). We also see that humanity consistently struggles between making work more or less significant than it should be in their lives. This tension is embedded in Genesis chapters 2 and 3 with the creation of work as a good and the corruption of work as a result of sin. Humanity seems to always be tempted toward one of two things: trying to draw more meaning out of work than it can give or to see work only as a necessary evil to acquire other goods in life.

The fourth and fifth relationships are closely connected. God saw that it was not good for the "man" to be alone and so he created a partner, "woman," to accompany him (2:18). As the author of Genesis records in the creation story of Eve, God paraded the land animals and the birds before Adam, and Adam named them (an important rite of authority in ancient cultures). In this process, it seems that God is doing two things, teaching Adam who he is and also making a sharp contrast between the animals and birds on one hand and Adam's partner on the other. Thus, relationship four is a proper relationship with oneself, knowing that we have a unique place in God's creation—different than the animals in that we are uniquely made in God's image, but different also than God in that we share a created kinship with the animals. Genesis 2:24 asserts that, in an idyllic state, man and woman were "naked and unashamed." This proper understanding of oneself again is affected by sin, when Adam and Eve recognize their "nakedness" and hide from the Lord (Gen 3:10).

Relationship five of an abundant life is the experience of meaningful relationships with other people. It was not good for man to be alone, so God created woman out of man to partner with him. The narrative of Genesis is a narrative of God forming a community of people, which will eventually extend through all the nations in the world, a community that he rules in kindness and holiness. This theme of extending God's blessings to the nations through Israel is God's common grace. Common grace is the kind of grace that is available to all people—it is not specific and particular to the people of God. "He [God] makes his sun rise on the evil and on the good, and sends rain on the righteous and on the unrighteous" (Matt 5:45). The Abrahamic covenant included a promise to bless all the nations through the covenant community of God, and again, the Pentateuch emphasizes a reason that the law was given: to demonstrate to the nations, through Israel as the carriers of the covenant, the wisdom and goodness of God (Deut 4:5–8). And as with the other three relationships, one's relationships with oneself and with other people are marred by the presence of sin. Alienation occurred on both fronts through a loss of innocence and a misguided self-perception—they perceived that they were naked and covered themselves (Gen 3:7). Moreover they proved a propensity to not take responsibility for their disobedience by blaming others (Gen 3:8–12).

The picture of life that the author of John paints, set in the context of the Hebrew understanding of life portrayed in the introductory chapters of Genesis, is multilayered. It stretches past the notion of eternal life to again use Willard's phrase, "an eternal kind of life." And this life consists of at least these five relationships: (1) with God, (2) with ourselves, (3) with others, (4) with the environment, and (5) with work. While a relationship with God seems to be the orienting center of these relationships, all five are important. We live in a relational kingdom.

These relationships get marred and fractured by sin and each can be corrupted in two directions. First, we can make too much out of a relationship and try to import more meaning into them than we should. This is a form of idolatry—"they exchanged the glory of the immortal God for images resembling a mortal human being or birds or four-footed animals . . . they exchanged the truth of God for a lie and worshiped and served the creature rather than the Creator" (Rom 1:23–25). For example, I live in Silicon Valley, where work is everything. If you are not working eighty hours per week and have a start-up company on the side, you really aren't keeping up. We pour too much meaning into our work, and it throws the other relationships out of rhythm. Second, we can make too little out of a particular relationship and try to diminish its importance. Evangelicals have been notoriously susceptible to this particular distortion of the importance of ecology in the life and witness of the church.[7]

7. Grudem, *Politics According to the Bible*.

When these five relationships are in the right rhythm, a kind of tension should be felt. This tension is affirming the goodness of the world in all that God created (that goodness is evident in all five relationships) and accounting for the reality that this goodness is no longer perfect because it has been corrupted by sin. Thus, there will be a pull in two directions: toward idolizing (setting a particular relationship over and above a relationship with God or beyond its own importance) or trivializing (not treating the relationship as important as it should be treated) in one or more of these areas. There is also the stark reality that, in a world corrupted by sin, the consequences of individual and institutional sin spin outward, having an incommensurate affect on the possibility of *shalom*. In Christian social ethics, this is where it is important to define the scriptural terms of "love" and "justice," because both concepts contribute to what it means for human beings to flourish. And, of course, both are mentioned numerous times in the Hebrew Scriptures as defining characteristics of God (1 John 4:8).

Love is the active contribution by one person to another in order to help these relationships flourish. I take the familiar passage of John 3:16—"For God so loved the world that he gave his only Son, so that everyone who believes in him may not perish, but have eternal life"—as precisely this in humanity's relationship with God, who is reaching toward human beings in love, through Jesus Christ, in order to initiate the redemptive process of reconciling humanity back to Godself. The Bible's great treatise on love is in 1 Corinthians 13:4–7: "Love is patient; love is kind; love is not envious or boastful or arrogant or rude. It does not insist on its own way; it is not irritable or resentful; it does not rejoice in wrongdoing, but rejoices in the truth. It bears all things, believes all things, hopes all things, endures all things." This is humanity's extension of God's love to one another. Glen Stassen calls this a "delivering love," a love that seeks the good of the other.[8] Similarly, justice is the active work of opposing those things that thwart human flourishing in these relationships—seeking to overcome the negative effects of sin. Reinhold Niebuhr argued that the ideal of love is important, but never achievable apart from God's benevolent love toward us. The best that human beings can do is approximate love through justice.[9] So justice is the social outworking of the ideal of the Christian virtue of love in practice. For Niebuhr, the ideal is important because it keeps human beings striving for more justice, but perfection is never achievable. Stassen argues that

8. Stassen and Gushee, *Kingdom Ethics*, 327–44.
9. Niebuhr, *Nature and Destiny of Man*, 246.

these two concepts are more closely tied together than Niebuhr's definitions allow and wants to work to bring them together: "Justice and love
must characterize all of a Christian's relationships."[10] Bringing these two
rich scriptural concepts together creates a new moral horizon that might
contribute to the kind of relationship between the church and the state that
I am trying to argue for. For the church, this is where the compassionate
impulses of love, the prophetic challenges of justice, and the creative experiments of a community inspired by the supererogatory virtue of loving
one's neighbor (and enemy) creates a different kind of posture toward the
state and the church's participation in the political.

I set out in chapter 2 to "mind the gap." I had originally thought that
the gap was a product of evangelical (especially white evangelicals) involvement in politics. This is true, but there is more to it. Politics is just an expression of power. Power is instrumental in social organization and is a part
of any governmental institution that is affirmed in the Scriptures, "[The
government] is God's servant to do you good . . . it is the servant of God
to execute wrath on the wrongdoer" (Rom 13:4). But power goes beyond
the political. Politics is the last resort when all other attempts at exercising
one's power to address a particular social issue have been exhausted. And
I want to connect the inclinations of the "Nones," and their desire for the
Christian tradition to return their attention and efforts on the community
described above, with the predisposition of the dominant evangelical community to focus the power they do have on politics. It seems to me that the
"Nones" are calling evangelicals to an authentic expression of their tradition by refocusing on the first word instead of the last. This is what I argued
in chapter 4. When Christianity puts its reasons in the public square and
hears criticisms of those reasons, their impact on particular communities,
and sees the visceral reactions (positive and negative), it has a prophetic
effect. It forces Christians to examine their sacred texts and accepted authorities and form or re-form an answer to epistemological challenges to
the veracity and existential experience of the Christian tradition. This kind
of challenge only produces a richer and more substantive faith tradition, or
it exposes a weakness.

In chapter 2, I tried to argue that the prophetic challenge of our day
has confronted the narrative of America as a "Christian Nation" that gives
Christians a privileged position at the table of public discourse. I maintain
that this idea was based on an inaccurate interpretation of Christianity's

10. Stassen and Gushee, *Kingdom Ethics*, 367.

sacred texts and a consequence of a misplaced analogy between the church and Israel. The Gospels and the letters in the New Testament speak of the community that is forming with Jesus at their center as an exilic community—aliens and strangers without a land, without a hereditary identifying marker and without a central place of worship—all by design. The church is now an international community that is salt and light; it is supposed to be one that does "good deeds" in whatever politic it finds itself. This seems to be what the "Nones" are asking of the church—to return to its roots for a more authentic expression of their faith.

Rodney Stark maintains that this was the impulse of the early church embedded in the ubiquity and tyranny of the Roman Empire. They kept on "doing good" in such a way that it created an ethos that eventually and incrementally changed an empire. Additionally, Stark's thesis articulates a contrast that I want to highlight between what it means to be a first-word Christian and a last-word Christian. This will work best if I give a historical example and contrast it with a contemporary situation.

Stark chronicles the Christian response to two plagues that swept through the Roman Empire in the second and third centuries CE—these plagues hit the densely populated cities the worst because the number and proximity of people in these cities intensified the rapid transfer of disease. It is estimated that about one quarter or one third of the entire population of the Roman Empire died during a fifteen-year span of the first epidemic. The common response to death and disease in these cities for those who had the means was to avoid contact and flee. Bodies were piled in the streets and the sick were abandoned as the plague devastated the people. Stark argues that the Christians were the ones who stayed and began to care for the sick and give proper burial for the deceased.[11] Their obligation to the sick and dying was grounded in the words of Jesus:

> For I was hungry and you gave me food, I was thirsty and you gave me something to drink, I was a stranger and you welcomed me, I was naked and you gave me clothing, I was sick and you took care of me, I was in prison and you visited me . . . just as you did it to one of the least of these who are members of my family, you did it to me. (Matt 25:35–36, 40)

Their obligation was also grounded in the works of Jesus—that he often touched those who would make him unclean according to ceremonial law, stooped to meet people in need, and had table fellowship with the outcasts.

11. Stark, *Triumph of Christianity*, location 1923.

Stark argues that this was a revolutionary idea that the traditional religious worldview of the Romans could not accommodate. There was no supererogatory extension of love and charity beyond one's own household: "if one went to a temple to pray, one discovered that the priests were not there praying for divine aid, but that all of them had fled the city . . . there was no belief that the gods cared about human affairs . . . the idea of a merciful or caring God was utterly alien."[12] The Christians who stayed back ended up caring for the sick and dying and saved numerous lives. This had an impact that stretched throughout the empire. Stark recounts the efforts of Emperor Julian (fourth century) to imitate Christian charity and mercy in the pagan priesthood: "[T]he impious Galileans [Christians], in addition to their own, support ours [and] it is shameful that our poor should be wanting our aid."[13] Christian love and charity was winsome and becoming the model for what is truly authentic religion.

Two points are important here. First, a sign of first-word Christianity is that it extends beyond the community of faith to the wider world without obligation or reward. Those that stayed to care for the sick and dying during both plagues often suffered the same fate as their neighbors. In a letter from Bishop Dionysius of Alexandria, the Bishop is quoted as describing the Christians' attitude, and ultimately their fate: "Heedless of danger, they took charge of the sick, attending to their every need and ministering to them in Christ, and with them departed this life serenely happy; for they were infected by others with the disease, drawing on themselves the sickness of their neighbors and cheerfully accepting their pains."[14] The second important sign of first-word Christianity is that the world looks upon the good that is done in Christ's name and tries to imitate it, to extend it further and often institutionalize a program to accomplish the same result. Stark quotes the emperor Julian's attempt to mimic the upstart Christian community to demonstrate when this happens. While the reasons go beyond a simple explanation, Stark hints that the efforts of the Christians during the plague had a positive impact on the lessening of the persecution of the church that began with Nero and contributed to the Christianization of the Roman Empire during Constantine's era. This idea of a "secular"

12. Ibid., 1904.

13. Ayer, *Source Book*, 332–33, as quoted in Stark, *Triumph of Christianity*, location 1959.

14. Dionysius, "Festival Letters," quoted in Eusebius, *History of the Church from Christ to Constantine*.

government taking the initiatives of the church's efforts to help meet the needs of the community, and trying to replicate them in wider society, is one of the marks that the church is getting the first-word idea right. Two more prominent examples of this in history are how Western medicine developed (out of these examples) and the importance of education. Both of these widespread practices started as works of Christian service that ended up as institutional goods to be distributed among all members of society.

I remember a lecture that an education professor gave in one of my undergraduate courses at Montana State University. She argued that the very idea of education in the Western World was complemented by the notion that every person needed to be able to read in order to understand the Bible and move toward salvation. In contrast to the Catholic Christian tradition that emphasized the mediated understanding of the Bible through the priests, the Protestant notion of the priesthood of all believers meant that everyone needed to be educated in order to be able to read and understand the Bible for oneself. Thus, despite the deleterious consequences of some Christian missionary efforts that were tied to Colonialism or Imperialism, one of the outcomes of missions around the world was that literacy rates increased wherever Christian mission work was present.[15]

Contrast this with a contemporary example of what it means to be last-word Christians. In 1981, several cases of *Pneumocystis carinii pneumonia* (PCP) were reported in large metropolitan cities. Several people died as a result of PCP, which later became identified as the Human Immunodeficiency Virus (HIV). HIV develops into Acquired Immunodeficiency Syndrome (AIDS), and an exponential number of people were dying of this disease. A crisis was developing. The communities that were most touched by this crisis were gay men and intravenous drug users. Within five years of its discovery, over thirty thousand Americans were diagnosed with AIDS.[16] The first care and service organization for people with AIDS—the Gay Men's Health Crisis—was established in 1981 by a few gay men in a living room in New York City to quell the fear of AIDS (and of gay men at that time). This organization still exists today and offers services to those with HIV and AIDS ranging from mental health counseling, providing vocational resources, and helping with meals for those in need.

15. For an example of this particular kind of influence on education, see Mantovanelli, "Protestant Legacy," http://economics.ucr.edu/seminars_colloquia/2013-14/economic_theory/Mantovanelli%20paper%20for%202%204%2014%20seminar.pdf.

16. Avert, "History of HIV and AIDS," http://www.avert.org/professionals/history-hiv-aids/overview.

In contrast to these early efforts, the evangelical Christian response to AIDS, at least in its public pronouncements, had a different quality altogether. Remember that this crisis surfaced concurrently with the peak stages of the religious right's support, backing, and election of Ronald Reagan. The Moral Majority had formed in 1979 and had catalyzed a wide range of support for their political strategy. The leader of the Moral Majority, Jerry Falwell, was at the apex of his popularity and influence in the evangelical community and the university that he founded—Liberty University—became a stop on any Republican presidential candidate's campaigns. Here are Falwell's words in response to the growing AIDS crisis and HIV epidemic in America: "AIDS is a lethal judgment of God on America for endorsing this vulgar, perverted and reprobate lifestyle."[17] Later, Falwell would double-down on this interpretation of the epidemic: "AIDS is the wrath of a just God against homosexuals. To oppose it would be like an Israelite jumping in the Red Sea to save one of Pharaoh's charioteers . . . AIDS is not just God's punishment for homosexuals; it is God's punishment for the society that tolerates homosexuals."[18] Similarly, Pat Robertson, the founder of the Christian Coalition, said this about AIDS in his speech to the Concerned Women of America:

> It is one of the most horrible things that is sweeping through our society. The blood supply is being polluted with this awful virus. And we're saying it's a civil rights matter. Those of us who do not engage in certain practices, such as intravenous drug use, etc., don't we have any rights? Don't we have any rights in America? Of course you have compassion for those who are sick. One of our staff sent me a memo just yesterday which said, in San Francisco, the victims of AIDS in the hospital who happen to be homosexual are given visiting rights in the hospital for their "lovers" to come into the hospital. They don't even let the heterosexuals do that.[19]

This kind of response—to declare that a particular disease, epidemic, or natural disaster is the judgment of God—has historical precedent. In the sixteenth century, one scholar described a plague as "the coming of the wrath of God, furious, sudden, swift, monstrous, dreadful."[20] The same

17. National Research Council (US), *Social Impact of AIDS*, 131.

18. McElvaine, *Grand Theft Jesus*, 35.

19. Robertson, "Concerned Citizens," http://www.patrobertson.com/speeches/ConcernedCitizens.asp.

20. Winslow, *Dwelling Place*, 177; National Research Council (US), *Social Impact of AIDS*, 125.

kind of rhetoric was used during the bubonic plague in London and the cholera epidemics in the United States.[21] The contrast in the two Christian responses (the cities in the Roman Empire and San Francisco) is striking. The Christians responded with care, compassion, and service to the plagues that ravaged the more densely populated places of the Roman Empire; the Christians in America (at least those that garnered the attention of the media) responded to the HIV/AIDS epidemic with fear and judgment. To be sure, there were important Christian efforts to care for the sick and dying in the cities where HIV/AIDS hit the hardest, but their quiet and consistent efforts were overshadowed as the political voices of the religious right got the bulk of attention. "Official statements, media reports, and other published accounts provide one source of information. Another source, perhaps a more important one, is beyond the easy reach of researchers: the history of personal attitudes and actions of individuals who are informed and motivated by religious beliefs."[22] It was not evangelicals who led the way in compassion and care during the HIV/AIDS crisis—the Catholic Church and the progressive branch of the Protestant tradition initiated programs to care for those who were dying. The Catholic Church's response is important because their call for ministry to the sick, dying, and bereaved in this instance cut across their theological convictions about sexuality. In 1984, the Diocese of San Jose issued this message:

> Ministry to the sick, dying and bereaved requires special attention and sensitivity in this context because the misunderstanding and hostility surrounding homosexuality has been grievously aggravated by the uncertainty and fear surrounding Acquired Immune Deficiency Syndrome. Afflicted individuals, their families and friends have a special claim on the ministry of the church.[23]

Glide Memorial United Methodist Church, an inclusive, progressive congregation located in the center of San Francisco is one of the notable congregations whose prescient work in ministering to the AIDS community is an example of progressive Protestants taking care of those most in need. Glide founded the Glide/Goodlet AIDS Project in 1989 and was one of the first churches in America to offer HIV testing at their church.[24] They continue to be a strong presence in the city of San Francisco today.

21. Ibid., 125–26.
22. Ibid.
23. Ibid.
24. Weatherford and Weatherford, *Somebody's Knocking at Your Door.*

The AIDS crisis, which coincided with the rise of the influence of the religious right—whether it was Jerry Falwell's Moral Majority or Pat Robertson's Christian Coalition—focused on having the last word, the political and judgmental word, as they interpreted the events that were unfolding in the early 1980s, and it set the LGBTQ community at odds with evangelicalism specifically, and also the broader stream of Christianity altogether. San Francisco has always been a place where those who did not fit into the mainstream of culture could find a place to belong, but the words of the evangelical leaders seem to communicate that the church was not one of those places. The consistent message was that HIV/AIDS is incompatible with the Christian faith. The residue of the impact of this movement is seen in the aforementioned 2008 statistics that characterized Christianity as primarily "anti-homosexual."[25]

There is also a contrast to be made in the responses to the subject of abortion—another divisive and hotly contested social issue. Part of the stated political platform of the religious right has always been preserving and protecting the sanctity of unborn life. Cathy Ruse, Senior Fellow for legal studies at the Family Research Council, recently reiterated the political strategy for stopping abortion in the 2016 American presidential election. She stated,

> The pro-life movement in America is stronger, more sophisticated, and younger than anywhere else on the planet. We know how to write legislation and how to get it passed at every level of government. We can bury Capitol Hill in post cards[sic] and shut down phone lines. We have learned how to find pro-life candidates, get them elected, and keep them accountable. We have become experts in adoption law and in real estate, opening thousands of pregnancy help centers, often right next door to the local abortion center. We have honed our media skills and even become investigative journalists, going undercover to expose the hideous realities behind that anodyne word "choice."
>
> But we have not been able to crack the ultimate lock: the Supreme Court.[26]

There are countless organizations outside of the political sphere that work to reduce the number of abortions worldwide (a goal of both pro-life and pro-choice advocates) but since the landmark Supreme Court case of *Roe v.*

25. Kinnaman and Lyons, *UnChristian*, 39.

26. Ruse, "What a Trump Court Would Mean," http://dailysignal.com/2016/11/29/what-a-trump-court-would-mean-for-abortion/.

Wade in 1973, the majority of attention seems to be focused on the political efforts to preserve or overturn that decision. The religious right has been at the center of that political conversation.

According to the Guttmacher Institute, the per capita abortion rates in the United States rose dramatically between 1973 and the early 1980s where they reached a peak of 29.3 of every 1000 women in 1981 (the criteria of the study were women between the ages of fifteen and forty-four who had an abortion). That number tapered off, then dramatically lowered between 2008 and 2011 to close to Roe-era levels of 16.9 of every 1000. Guttmacher points out that this decline predates a surge in legislative efforts that began again in 2011. It is difficult to isolate the causal factors in this decline, but there a few aspects that should be considered. 2008 marked a worldwide recession that affected the economy. Birth rates also declined during this period, and it is certainly reasonable to think that poor economic circumstances breed caution in procreative decisions. Concurrently, the advances of scientific understanding of fetal development continues to reveal the complexity of human development in the womb, which seems to have bearing on what kinds of restrictions might be warranted as a pregnancy develops: "This is a post-sonogram generation . . . There is increased awareness throughout our culture of the moral weight of the unborn baby. And that's a good thing."[27]

One factor that is hard to isolate, but has some historical precedent is that abortion rates have dropped as the acuity of the political conversation for the religious right turned from abortion to same-sex marriage. Massachusetts passed the first law legalizing same-sex marriage in 2003. Between 2003 and 2015, when the Supreme Court decided that gay couples have a constitutional right to the institution of marriage and its subsequent rights, thirty-seven states and the District of Columbia had legalized same-sex marriage and thirteen states had put bans into practice.[28] My purpose here is not to debate the merits of same-sex marriage, but to draw attention to the shift in legislative focus by evangelicals. For example, in 2004, James Dobson formed Focus on the Family Action—a political organization created to combat the increasing pressure to legalize same-sex marriage. Dobson said, "The attack and assault on marriage is so distressing that I just feel

27. Somashekhar, "Study: Abortion Rate," https://www.washingtonpost.com/national/health-science/study-abortion-rate-at-lowest-point-since-1973/2014/02/02/8dea007c-8a9b-11e3-833c-33098f9e5267_story.html.

28. "State Same-Sex Marriage," http://www.governing.com/gov-data/same-sex-marriage-civil-unions-doma-laws-by-state.html.

like I can't remain silent."[29] Contrast this with James Hunter's admonition mentioned earlier, that Christians should remain silent for a season until they can learn to talk in a non-Nietzschean manner. How do these two competing ideas coexist?

In the mid-1800s, the abortion rate per capita in the United States ran parallel to contemporary statistics. There was also a political skirmish being waged over the legality of abortion—those who were advocating against abortion were mostly doctors trying to prevent unlicensed persons from performing medical procedures. While the merits of legalized abortions were being debated in the political arena (without much church involvement), religious folks were working outside of the political machinations to create structures to support women with unwanted pregnancies. Adoption agencies were created, single and young mother's poverty was being addressed, and orphans were taken in. By some estimates, these efforts dramatically reduced the number of abortions being performed (almost by half).[30] Conservative scholar Marvin Olasky maintains that this was the compassion of predominantly "faith-based" organizations like the Florence Crittenton Mission, the Home for Fallen and Friendless Girls, and the Erring Woman's Refuge that contributed to the decrease of the abortion rates in the 1800s.[31] He goes on to argue that, in the early twentieth century, these efforts were secularized and professionalized in a way that decreased their effectiveness in providing an alternative to ending an unwanted pregnancy. Again, this is an example of the culture trying to imitate successful social programs initiated by the church.

This kind of unique and creative work of the church in culture is an example of what it means to be first-word Christians. It is attempting to bring the depth of faith, the practices of the tradition, and the creativity of those who express a commitment to faith in God to bear on some of the most important social issues of the day. William Willimon recounts a story of a fourteen-year-old girl who was unprepared for raising a child and what it would be like to become a mother. The African-American minister of the congregation of which she was a part baptized the baby and challenged the congregation to help raise the mother and the child. The baby was taken in by a retired couple who had demonstrated in their own parenting

29. Kirkpatrick, "Warily, a Religious Leader," http://www.nytimes.com/2004/05/13/us/2004-campaign-evangelical-christians-warily-religious-leader-lifts-his-voice.html.

30. Thomas and Dobson, *Blinded by Might*, 98, 99.

31. Olasky and Bennett, *Abortion Rites*, 197–217.

experience to be relatively successful at raising children. They were asked to not only raise the baby, but also help the mother as well.[32]

There are numerous small examples of faith-based organizations creatively and compassionately addressing the needs of their particular communities as part of the normal rhythm and practice of their congregations. I put out a request for stories like these through social media, and several people wrote to describe the programs that their churches have developed or are in the process of developing. One church in New York State is helping to settle Nepalese refugees who are fleeing Bhutan. First Presbyterian Church in Berkeley has redesigned a portion of their church to create a coffee shop to help train Syrian refugees as baristas and provide entry-level jobs as they begin to form new lives in the United States. First Presbyterian Church in Pomona (one-hundred-person membership) has been mentoring underserved and at-risk children for twenty years, and out of that helped create a nonprofit called Pomona New Hope. There is a small but similar organization started by a Lutheran Church in Wilton North Dakota. My own church has several initiatives for the homeless and the underserved communities in the San Francisco Bay Area. These stories are almost as numerous as American churches themselves. It is a small cross-section of those people who are filling the gaps in what the formal institutions of government can and cannot do. And these programs do not rely on the sponsorship of the government in most cases—they are independent initiatives that promote the welfare and flourishing of members in the community.

I want to conclude this chapter by comparing two "declarations" that illustrate the kind of posture for which I am arguing: The Barmen Declaration of the Confessing Church, which was written in 1934 and was meant to address the rising tide of Nazism, and the Manhattan Declaration, written by an ecumenical group of independent Christians seeking to address the "moral drift" of America in the twenty-first century. The Manhattan Declaration begins by affirming the richness of the Christian tradition and the moral good that it has done in Western culture for two thousand years: "Christians are heirs of a 2,000-year tradition of proclaiming God's word, seeking justice in our societies, resisting tyranny, and reaching out with compassion to the poor, oppressed and suffering."[33] It acknowledges (very quickly and almost dismissively) the injustice, fostering tyranny, and being

32. Willimon, *What's Right with the Church*, 71.
33. "Manhattan Declaration," http://manhattandeclaration.org/index.html.

the oppressors of the poor and marginalized. "While fully acknowledging the imperfections and shortcomings of Christian institutions and communities in all ages, we claim the heritage of those Christians who defended innocent life by rescuing discarded babies from trash heaps in Roman cities and publicly denouncing the Empire's sanctioning of infanticide." It goes on to focus on three core issues: life, marriage, and freedom of religion, and argues for government leaders to affirm life in all circumstances (save the death penalty), affirm traditional marriage, and maintain freedom of religion. The Manhattan Declaration is a clarion call for the government to support a select few important moral issues because the consequences are dire for a once-moral Western world.

In contrast, the Barmen Declaration is anchored by seven theological rejections—"we reject the false doctrine of"—that are directed toward the church in Germany. In this way, the focus is not on the nation-state of Germany (although the drafters of the Barmen Declaration affirm their loyalty to Germany) but on the return of the church to faithfulness to Jesus Christ. For the authors, a true expression of the Christian tradition in Germany would benefit Germany: "In view of the errors of the 'German Christians' of the present Reich Church government which are devastating the Church and also therefore breaking up the unity of the German Evangelical Church, we confess the following evangelical truths."[34]

The contrast between these two declarations highlights the emphasis of this chapter (and the theme of this book). The focus of religious groups in a pluralistic public square should be placed squarely on the authenticity of their own tradition. As statistics have demonstrated, even those that do not consider themselves religious seem to know that the first-word impulse that Walzer describes—the more creative and interesting word—is an authentic expression of the Christian tradition. Something seems off, triumphalistic, and imperialistic when the best resources of the church—human, creative, financial, etc.—are primarily directed toward the political sphere. I've tried to highlight just a few historical cases that support this argument. When the church relies on political power to achieve its social goals, it is often disappointed. Conservative commentator Cal Thomas aptly summarizes the consequences of this misplaced hope:

> This power has nothing to do with government and even less to do with politics. We seem to be asking the government and politics to do for us what we should be doing for ourselves. If we succumb

34. Barth, "Theological Declaration of Barmen," 8.09.

to the lure of a government "Quick fix" and absolve ourselves of
personal responsibility, we will be no better (and not better off)
than the big-government liberals we so often criticize for turning
to government as a first resource and not as a last resort.[35]

This is Thomas's mea culpa from years of involvement in the formation of
the Moral Majority and its political agenda. In the end, he returned to the
idea that participation in politics is important but not ultimate; the emphasis of the community of faith that follows Jesus should be on recovering its
uniqueness as the church. There are creative congregants waiting for the
opportunity to express the authenticity of their Christian faith, but have
worried that to focus their efforts on the political seems misguided. And
there are those who stand outside of the Christian faith who are longing to
see those congregants focus on the flourishing of their communities and
invest their times, talents, and treasure toward those ends.

35. Thomas and Dobson, *Blinded by Might*, 32.

Conclusion

WE LIVE IN MULTIPLE traditions; this is the essence of a post-secular age. No one tradition dominates (whether secular or religious), and people are searching for a bigger story to understand the meaning and significance of our lives in this context. Cornel West calls this the "tragicomic" reality of life. West's unique blending of the expansion of democracy with the imagery, symbolism, metaphor, and lessons from Jesus help to shape his argument for "radical democracy," a democracy that draws people in from the margins, and a "prophetic Christianity," a faith that recognizes and empathizes with the suffering of the "least of these."[1] This is the kind of prophetic relationship between the democratic and the Christian tradition for which I am trying to argue. West is cautious about the possibilities of an idealized democratic tradition that is unresponsive to the voices of the marginalized. The kind that does not recognize that when you begin to argue for a romantic notion of democracy, those arguments draw on resources and ideas from another tradtion. I argued something similar in chapter 3: that the democratic tradition is a thin tradition that needs a complement to produce citizens of virtue. And I don't think that the exclusion of religious voices, reason, and practices from the public square for the sake of a "sacred" securalism is the answer. To isolate religious beliefs and practices to the purely personal realm in favor of a sanitized public square is to minimize some of the very things that bring democracy's citizens the most meaning. It is no wonder that secular democracies tend to see an upsurge in traditional religious pushback after a generation of development.[2]

West also argues that American democracy has a unique problem: historical amnesia. We move too quickly to give a promissory note of hope

1. West, *Cornel West Reader*, xviii.
2. See Walzer, *The Paradox of Liberation*.

and possibility without acknowledging or addressing the injustices of the past.[3] For West, the complement to the democratic tradition that I argued for in chapter 3 is a distinctive type of Christianity. West is by no means a conservative evangelical; he is a self-described "Checkovian Christian" that melds the sympathies of the great Russian novelists (especially Anton Checkov) with the legacy of the black church in America. This is where he develops the idea of "tragicomedy": "The tragedy is that we are constrained in our freedom by limits we are not aware of and the comedy is acknowledging those limitations and the 'incongruity' between [our] high aspirations and where one actually ends up."[4] For West, Jesus is the center of this tragicomic storm—an incarnation of God in the suffering reality of humanity. And Jesus' teachings expand our moral boundaries outward to "the least of these" in society.

I have focused this book on the relationship between Christianity and democracy for three reasons: First, Christianity is my own tradition and I am concerned that the ways we as evangelicals think about the relationship between Christianity and democracy have been misguided, and it has produced some tragic consequences. So I want to be a part of the conversation to try to recover the prophetic tension between the two traditions that produces a richer and more textured Christian faith and a more inclusive democracy. Second, Christianity and democracy have had a unique history together in Western Culture. That history has been muddled by the evangelical church's efforts to control the levers of cultural power and subsequent counterefforts to restrain religion from overstepping its boundaries. This is politics—the efforts to bring diverse groups of people together into some kind of cooperative social organization are rarely tidy. Further, the real possibility and history of religious violence done in the name of Christianity has obscured the prophetic voice of the Christian tradition, and at other times a drift toward secularism to correct that problem has resulted in marginalizing religious voices—both responses fester at the extreme edges of each tradition. But I have tried to describe a way in which these two great traditions can relate together for the good of the community. This way is prophetic in the best sense of the term, calling each tradition to be faithful to their core beliefs, text, and authorities, so a tension between them needs to be present. One tradition cannot reign hegemonic over the other. Third, I think that, at its best, the Christian tradition has the resources to

3. West, *Cornel West Reader*, xx.
4. Ibid., 557.

CONCLUSION

complement the democratic tradition, and that democracy has been good for Christianity. I argued that Christianity complements democracy in two ways: (1) Its supererogatory command of loving one's neighbor (and one's enemies) brings those that democracy naturally marginalizes into focus: "They [Christians] busy themselves on earth, but their citizenship is in heaven. They obey the laws of the land but in their own lives go far beyond the laws' requirements."[5] (2) Christianity is a "red-hot poker" in the soul of democracy.[6] Democratic politics is about compromise, the majority, and the relative social conventions and social *mores* of the day; Christianity is absolutist, the minority, and concerned with the universal reality of living one's life as a follower of Jesus. Those two together can be combustible, but they can also create a crucible for refining one another's harder edges.

To bring these two traditions together in this kind of refining, prophetic relationship, I have argued that the democratic tradition needs to rethink the relationship between church and state. Democracy is uniquely suited to accommodate our increasing pluralism. It elevates each individual and community by offering the hope of having a say in one's own life plans. It creates room for individuals to experiment and make corrections along the way. And, ideally, it values everyone's contribution to determine the goods of society and how those goods get distributed. Democracy also has a minimal mechanism for the minority voice—the freedom to express one's dissent in voluntary and secondary associations that support a life plan that might run counter to the utilitarian calculations of the good by the majority. Within the broad boundaries of separation that I outlined in chapter 1, there is a lot of blank canvas to fill with creative solutions to some of our most pressing social problems—and that space should not be limited to only the non-religious. In chapter 1, I called this an "art" because it takes a kind of fuzziness, or blur, to create the space for people to bring their religious ideas, reasons, and practices to the public conversation. To prejudice the public square against this kind of religious creativity is to miss out on the opportunity to develop something new. West describes the benefits of prophetic Christianity in this way:

5. Richardson, "Epistle to Diognetus," 216–18; quoted in Willimon, *What's Right with the Church*.

6. Grubb, *C. T. Studd*. This is how C. T. Studd described his wife, as told by Norman P. Grubb in *C. T. Studd: Cricketeer and Pioneer*, and I thought that it was an apt metaphor for the relationship between Christianity and democracy.

Its synoptic vision speaks with insight and power to the multiform character of human existence and to the specificity of the historical modes of human existence. Its moral vision and ethical norms propel human intellectual activity to account for and transform existing forms of dogmatism, oppression, and despair.[7]

For West, the relationship between Christianity and democracy is like jazz: improvising our way through to produce something beautiful for all people. It is experimental and requires the best that its citizens have to offer—even its religious citizens.

I think that it is wise for the democratic tradition to open the boundaries of public discourse much wider because it can offer layers of texture to the tradition. It is also wise because if a group (what I've been calling secondary or voluntary associations that make up civil society) is necessarily excluded from the conversation, it will produce frustration that will seek some kind of outlet. The promissory note of democracy is the hope that everyone has an opportunity to determine his or her own life plan, and if someone is excluded, this produces dissonance. While I have tried to steer clear of most specific references to the 2016 political climate in America and the election of Donald Trump, it is clear that Trump's victory is anchored in this kind of frustration (whether justified or not) in white evangelicals and the rural poor. Opening the boundaries of the democratic tradition might mute some of these frustrations.

This might be an acceptable conclusion if we were creating democracy from a blank slate and could negotiate freshly the relationship between religion and democracy. But we have a history in Western culture, an institutional memory, that causes us to worry about trotting religion out in the public square again. It seems like we have tried that and found it wanting. This is what I argued in the introduction: a fondness for and attraction to the spiritual is a way to center the meaning in one's life—it acknowledges something beyond us that might tie our experiences together. At the same time, there is a reticence to identify with any particular religious tradition because of religious conflict. This is a kind of personal syncretism that tries to avoid the pitfalls of religious history while retaining its spiritual essence. It is precisely at this point that I tried to argue that the democratic tradition has had a prophetic role in the moral formation of Christianity.

John Howard Yoder calls the fourth-century Roman adoption of Christianity as the official religion of the empire the "Constantinian

7. West, *Cornel West Reader*, 371.

CONCLUSION

compromise." Yoder maintains that the church compromised its integrity and was baptized into the secular power equation. Without rehearsing the negative and positive influences of Christendom on the West and the world, we can say that the posture of the church changed as a consequence of wedding Christian faith with the empire. I have argued that the corollary of this change in posture is that the church exchanged New Testament metaphors of exiles, strangers, and aliens in the relationship between Rome and the followers of Jesus for metaphors of theocratic Israel—where God is the legislator, and obedience and faithfulness to the Mosaic covenant secured blessings for the nation of Israel. It is easy to imagine how any marginalized group of people might pick up the story of the suffering of the Israelites as slaves in Egypt and draw an analogy to their own suffering and hoped-for deliverance. It also does not take much effort to then move toward that vision of a "promised land" and a new life. This was the Puritan impulse in the early colonial days and remains an evangelical impulse today: to equate America with Israel and then to look to theocratic images when cultural tides shift away from "biblical *mores*."

In chapter 4, I claimed that democracy has played a prophetic role to Christianity in the West. Because Christianity has been the dominant tradition, because it is absolutist, and because it is a natural human inclination to "conserve" one's power if you have it, the Christian tradition wedded with any empire can fall prey to hegemony. Democracy's thin ethic of harm, its promise to allow people to develop their own life plan, and its common language of rights embedded an epistemological challenge to Christianity: what group of people is being excluded in the Christian vision of a just social order? This is not a new challenge. This was the very challenge of Jesus in the pages of the gospels as he ate with "tax collectors and sinners" (Matthew 9:11), had conversations with Gentiles and women (the woman at the well in John 4), and stated that what his disciples did for the prisoner, the poor, and the outcast, they did for him (Matthew 25). The clamor for new rights in a pluralistic public square is a constant epistemological challenge for the Christian tradition to return to its sacred beliefs, texts, and authorities, and see if they need to be adjusted (or our interpretation of them needs to be adjusted) in order to be what Hunter calls a "faithful presence." This is true in historical examples like slavery, miscegenation laws, women's rights, and even the idea of freedom of religion. It is also true in the contemporary questions of LGBTQ rights, immigration reform, and growing environmental concerns.

I argued that the exchange of exilic images for theocratic images of Israel, the enculturated Christian faith that accompanies nationalism, and the nostalgic longings for Christian America (or the Christian foundations of America), should all be jettisoned in favor of a return to exile, a prophetic critique of national self-interest, and a longing for a distinct kind of faith that stands out in culture. This does not mean that Christians cannot affirm the good that any state or culture is doing, but that in affirming it, they can connect that good with values that are rooted in the picture of the kingdom of God that is painted in the New Testament and the hope for the deliverance of God in the Hebrew Scriptures. This seems to be what the admonitions toward submission to the governing authorities affirms— participation in politics is part of what it means for Christians to be both lowercase "c" citizens of a particular country, and uppercase "C" citizens of the kingdom of God. Politics is important, but not ultimate. In contrast, where the nation-state or any institution of governmental authority has reversed its role and is promoting evil and punishing good, Christians must participate by prophetically speaking into this situation, and must face the consequences of swimming against the current of cultural trends.

This idea is animated and captured best by Michael Walzer's conclusion that the "saints have what is more interesting: the first word. They set the stage of history for the new order."[8] I've argued that the Christian tradition would be strengthened (and democracy would be stronger) if Christianity recovered this first word impulse. It was this quotation by Walzer in my early research that captured my attention. I thought that Walzer was right; that there is much to be gained if the church can harness its creativity toward initiating and implementing new ideas or programs to help meet the needs of their community—to promote their neighbors' flourishing. This has been practiced in specific historical situations, and is taking place in current iterations that regularly go unnoticed (except by those who benefit from these programs). This kind of creativity comes more naturally when you sit at the margins of the conversation (in exile) than if you are at the center of power. Creativity comes when you have to find another way to accomplish your goals than through coercion. You can see this in the traditions of the black church, which develops programs for both their parishioners and their community to combat injustice and overcome the obstacles of racism. The black church has traditionally been a community in exile and on the underside of power in America, and white evangelicals

8. Walzer, *Revolution of the Saints*, 319.

can learn from the black church in this way. You can also see this in the peace church tradition. When you cannot settle personal disputes with violence or international disputes with war, it forces you to come up with creative solutions for conflict resolution and peacemaking efforts.

This seems to be where we are in politics: our lack of a common moral framework and language to settle disputes about the good sets the inevitable conflict of democracy into a heightened state. There is no way to resolve differences except through the assertion of power so there is less and less bipartisanship. My argument is that evangelicals traded in their creativity for a place at the power table. This is why James Hunter can say, "Christians should remain silent for a season, until we can learn how to talk about politics in a non-Nietzschean manner." Hunter never quite says it this way, but his argument is that we need to recover the uniqueness of the church and its faithfulness to Christ as a politic itself. This is an argument that Yoder, Hauerwas, and others have made: the church has cozied up to power, and it has cost them their witness in Western culture. This is a theological argument, but as I pointed to in the work of Cal Thomas, a few of the charter members of the religious right have argued that looking back, the focused efforts of playing politics as a means toward Christian ends backfired. This is a practical argument and begs for a new way.

I have argued that the Christian Scriptures assume the ubiquity of Rome and its autocratic presence, and present a fairly simple charge to the church in this context: governmental institutions are a way for God to distribute God's common grace to all people and to keep order in society. They are a flawed institution that is supposed to promote human flourishing. Sometimes they get it right, and sometimes wrong. The church is to recognize this as a gift of God and work within it—in submission (Rom 13, 1 Pet 2)—for their own good and the good of others. This submission means participation without placing our ultimate hope in governments. It means recognizing the flawed and corrupted nature of even the best intentions, prophetically affirming where a government institution gets it right, and prophetically (and non-violently) speaking against it when it is not promoting good. But it means more than that. The church's hope is in something greater than what any governmental institution can establish, and that is what we work toward—we promote and pray for the welfare of the "city," because the church has a bigger picture of what it means for human beings to flourish. I argued that the posture of exile requires finding the practices of faithfulness to Christ in each culture, striving toward excellence in our work, and recovering the compassion and creativity that marked the early church. This was the emphasis of exilic stories in the Hebrew Scriptures, and marks similar contemporary examples. There is not a prescription for how this works (i.e., "follow these four steps"), and that's why the title of chapter 6 is "Experiments in Exile." It takes initiative, failure, re-learning, and more initiative to come up with appropriate means to promote the flourishing or our communities. The church will not always get it right the first time, but there should be an expectation that the church should keep trying.

Because sound-bite politics often gets the attention in the media, and the salacious overwhelms the subtle, this kind of work often goes unnoticed. Christians are not supposed to do good for the attention they might receive or with conditions, but are to do it sacrificially. There are many instances in the pages of the gospels where Jesus does something for someone and then tells them not to mention this to anyone. The church's posture in relationship to the political workings of any government should start with a faith centered on Jesus Christ, hope in something greater than the government that allows for prophetic participation, and a supereragatory love that is sacrificial and sets the church at the boundaries of inclusion. These are the cardinal virtues of Christian faith defined in 1 Corinthians 13. This is the place in which the church should be participating in their "Experiments in Exile." When the church embodies this first-word impulse with creativity and compassion, those outside the faith can recognize the goodness, and possibly hear the gospel for a "second time" in Western culture. It seems that this is what they want to see out of the Christian faith, and it is where the best moral moments of the Christian tradition have taken place.

Bibliography

Alexander, Michelle. *The New Jim Crow: Mass Incarceration in the Age of Colorblindness.* New York: New Press, 2010.

Ayer, Joseph Cullen. *A Source Book for Ancient Church History: From the Apostolic Age to the Close of the Conciliar Period.* New York: Scribner's, 1913.

Barth, Karl. "Declaration of Barmen." http://www.sacred-texts.com/chr/barmen.htm.

Beilby, James K, and Paul R. Eddy. *The Nature of the Atonement: Four Views.* Downers Grove, IL: IVP Academic, 2006.

Berlin, Adele, et al., eds. *The Jewish Study Bible: Jewish Publication Society Tanakh Translation.* Oxford: Oxford University Press, 2004.

Bethge, Eberhard. *Dietrich Bonhoeffer: A Biography.* Revised and edited by Victoria J. Barnett. Translated by Eric Mosbacher, et al. Minneapolis: Fortress, 2000.

Black, Edwin. *War Against the Weak: Eugenics and America's Campaign to Create a Master Race.* Expanded edition. Washington, DC: Dialog, 2012.

Bonhoeffer, Dietrich. *Christ the Center.* Translated by Edwin Robertson. San Francisco: HarperOne, 2009.

Buck, Christopher. *Religious Myths and Visions of America: How Minority Faiths Redefined America's World Role.* Westport, CT: Praeger, 2009.

"Buck v. Bell." Legal Information Institute. https://www.law.cornell.edu/supremecourt/text/274/200.

Campolo, Tony. "For the Record." *Tony Campolo,* June 8, 2015. http://tonycampolo.org/for-the-record-tony-campolo-releases-a-new-statement/#.WHGPRDu7pSU.

Campus Crusade for Christ. "Campus Crusade for Christ Adopts New Name: Cru." *PR Newswire,* July 19, 2011. http://www.prnewswire.com/news-releases/campus-crusade-for-christ-adopts-new-name-cru-125862368.html.

Churchill, Winston. *Churchill by Himself: The Definitive Collection of Quotations.* Edited by Richard Langworth. New York: PublicAffairs, 2008.

Cladis, M. S. "Painting Landscapes of Religion in America: Four Models of Religion in Democracy." *Journal of the American Academy of Religion* 76 (2008) 874–904. doi: 10.1093/jaarel/lfn088.

Claiborne, Shane, and Chris Haw. *Jesus for President: Politics for Ordinary Radicals.* Grand Rapids: Zondervan, 2008.

"Declaration of Independence: A Transcription." *National Archives.* https://www.archives.gov/founding-docs/declaration-transcript.

BIBLIOGRAPHY

"Dred Scott v. Sandford: Primary Documents of American History (Virtual Programs & Services, Library of Congress)." https://www.loc.gov/rr/program/bib/ourdocs/DredScott.html.

Eusebius of Caesarea. *The History of the Church from Christ to Constantine*. Translated by G. A Williamson. New York: Dorset, 1984.

Findlay, Gwyneth. "Wolterstorff Says 'Yes' to Same-Sex Marriage." *Calvin College Chimes*, October 21, 2016. http://www.calvin.edu/chimes/2016/10/22/wolterstorff-says-yes-to-same-sex-marriage/.

Fortanet, Joaquin, and Jennifer Rosato. "Pragmatism and Democracy: An Interview of Richard Rorty." *Journal of Philosophical Research* 34 (2009) 1–5. doi: 10.5840/jpr_2009_4.

Friesen, Duane K. *Artists, Citizens, Philosophers: Seeking the Peace of the City: An Anabaptist Theology of Culture*. Scottdale, PA: Herald, 2000.

Futato, Mark. "Because It Had Rained: A Study of Gen 2:5–7 with Implications for Gen 2:4–25 and Gen 1:1—2:3." *Westminster Theological Journal* 60 (1998) 1–21.

Grubb, Norman P. *C. T. Studd: Cricketer & Pioneer*. Fort Washington, PA: Christian Literature Crusade, 1982.

Grudem, Wayne A. *Politics According to the Bible: A Comprehensive Resource for Understanding Modern Political Issues in Light of Scripture*. Grand Rapids: Zondervan, 2010.

———. "Why Voting for Donald Trump Is a Morally Good Choice (Part 1)." *The Christian Post*, July 30, 2016. http://www.christianpost.com/news/why-voting-for-donald-trump-is-a-morally-good-choice-part-1-167239/.

Gushee, David P. *The Future of Faith in American Politics: The Public Witness of the Evangelical Center*. Waco: Baylor University Press, 2008.

Habermas, Jürgen. "Notes on a Post-Secular Society." *Sign and Sight*, June 18, 2008. www.signandsight.com/features/1714.html.

Harrell, Fred, et al. "A Letter from the Elder Board." https://www.citychurchsf.org/A-Letter-From-The-Elder-Board.

Hauerwas, Stanley. *After Christendom? How the Church Is to Behave if Freedom, Justice, and a Christian Nation Are Bad Ideas*. Nashville: Abingdon, 1991.

———. *Against the Nations: War and Survival in a Liberal Society*. Minneapolis: Winston, 1985.

———. *A Community of Character: Toward a Constructive Christian Social Ethic*. Notre Dame: University of Notre Dame Press, 1981.

———. *In Good Company: The Church as Polis*. Notre Dame: University of Notre Dame Press, 1995.

Hauerwas, Stanley, and Romand Coles. *Christianity, Democracy, and the Radical Ordinary: Conversations Between a Radical Democrat and a Christian*. Eugene, OR: Cascade, 2008.

Hauerwas, Stanley, and William H. Willimon. *Resident Aliens: Life in the Christian Colony*. Nashville: Abingdon, 1989.

"History of HIV and AIDS." https://www.avert.org/professionals/history-hiv-aids/overview.

Hughes, Richard T. *Myths America Lives By*. Urbana: University of Illinois Press, 2004.

Hunter, James Davison. *Culture Wars: The Struggle to Control the Family, Art, Education, Law, And Politics in America*. New York: Basic, 1991.

———. *To Change the World: The Irony, Tragedy, and Possibility of Christianity in the Late Modern World*. New York: Oxford University Press, 2010.

Hynes, Patrick. *In Defense of the Religious Right: Why Conservative Christians Are the Lifeblood of the Republican Party and Why That Terrifies the Democrats*. Nashville: Thomas Nelson, 2006.

"Jefferson's Wall of Separation Letter." http://www.usconstitution.net/jeffwall.html.

"John F. Kennedy Quotations: President Kennedy's Inaugural Address, January 20th, 1961." https://www.jfklibrary.org/Research/Research-Aids/Ready-Reference/JFK-Quotations/Inaugural-Address.aspx.

Jones, Robert P. *The End of White Christian America*. New York: Simon & Schuster, 2016.

Karslake, Daniel G. *For the Bible Tells Me So*. Documentary, 2007.

Keith, Heather, and Kenneth D. Keith. *Intellectual Disability: Ethics, Dehumanization and a New Moral Community*. Chichester, UK: Wiley-Blackwell, 2013.

Keller, Timothy J. "Serving the City." http://www.gospelinlife.com/serving-the-city-9274.

"King Papers." http://okra.stanford.edu/transcription/document_images/undecided/630 416-019.pdf.

King, Martin Luther, Jr. "I Have a Dream." http://www.thekingcenter.org/archive/document/i-have-dream-1.

———. *Strength to Love*. Minneapolis: Fortress, 1994.

Kinnaman, David, and Gabe Lyons. *UnChristian: What a New Generation Really Thinks About Christianity—and Why It Matters*. Grand Rapids: Baker, 2007.

Kirkpatrick, David D. "Warily, a Religious Leader Lifts His Voice in Politics." *New York Times*, May 13, 2004. http://www.nytimes.com/2004/05/13/us/2004-campaign-evangelical-christians-warily-religious-leader-lifts-his-voice.html.

Levine, Amy-Jill, and Marc Zvi Brettler, eds. *The Jewish Annotated New Testament: New Revised Standard Version*. Oxford: Oxford University Press, 2011.

Lincoln, Abraham. "Second Inaugural Address of Abraham Lincoln." http://avalon.law.yale.edu/19th_century/lincoln2.asp.

Lombardo, Paul A., ed. *A Century of Eugenics in America: From the Indiana Experiment to the Human Genome Era*. Bloomington: Indiana University Press, 2011.

MacIntyre, Alasdair C. *After Virtue: A Study in Moral Theory*. Notre Dame: University of Notre Dame Press, 1984.

———. *Three Rival Versions of Moral Enquiry: Encyclopedaedia, Genealogy, and Tradition*. Notre Dame, IN: University of Notre Dame Press, 1990.

———. *Whose Justice? Which Rationality?* Notre Dame: University of Notre Dame Press, 1988.

"Manhattan Declaration." http://manhattandeclaration.org/index.html.

Mantovanelli, Federico G. "The Protestant Legacy: Missions and Literacy in India." http://economics.ucr.edu/seminars_colloquia/2013-14/economic_theory/Mantovanelli%20paper%20for%202%204%2014%20seminar.pdf.

Marsden, George M. *The Soul of the American University: From Protestant Establishment to Established Nonbelief*. New York: Oxford University Press, 1994.

———. *The Twilight of the American Enlightenment: The 1950s and the Crisis of Liberal Belief*. New York: Basic, 2014.

McElvaine, Robert S. *Grand Theft Jesus: The Hijacking of Religion in America*. New York: Broadway, 2009.

McLennan, Scotty. *Christ for Unitarian Universalists: A New Dialogue with Traditional Christianity*. Boston: Skinner, 2016.

Bibliography

————. *Finding Your Religion: When the Faith You Grew Up With Has Lost Its Meaning.* San Francisco: HarperSanFrancisco, 1999.

————. *Jesus Was a Liberal: Reclaiming Christianity for All.* New York: St. Martin's Griffin, 2010.

Metaxas, Eric. "Should Christians Vote for Trump?" *Wall Street Journal,* October 12, 2016. http://www.wsj.com/articles/should-christians-vote-for-trump-1476294992.

Mohler, Albert. "Should We Be Patriots in the Pew?" *AlbertMohler.com,* July 3, 2008. http://www.albertmohler.com/2008/07/03/should-we-be-patriots-in-the-pew/.

Moore, Russell. *Onward: Engaging the Culture without Losing the Gospel.* Nashville: B & H, 2015.

National Research Council (US). *The Social Impact of AIDS in the United States.* Edited by Albert R. Jonsen and Jeff Stryker. Washington, DC: National Academies Press, 1993.

Needleman, Jason. "The American Soul: Rediscovering the Wisdom of the Founders." New York: Penguin, 2003.

Newport, Frank. "Majority Still Says Religion Can Answer Today's Problems." *Gallup.com,* June 27, 2014. http://www.gallup.com/poll/171998/majority-says-religion-answer-today-problems.aspx.

Niebuhr, H. Richard. *Christ and Culture.* New York: Harper, 1951.

Niebuhr, Reinhold. *The Nature and Destiny of Man: A Christian Interpretation.* New York: Scribner, 1964.

Noll, Mark A. *The Civil War as a Theological Crisis.* Chapel Hill: University of North Carolina Press, 2006.

————. *The Scandal of the Evangelical Mind.* Grand Rapids: Eerdmans, 1994.

Olasky, Marvin, and William J. Bennett. *Abortion Rites: A Social History of Abortion in America.* Wheaton, IL: Crossway, 1992.

Ortberg, John. *Who Is This Man? The Unpredictable Impact of the Inescapable Jesus.* Reprint edition. Grand Rapids: Zondervan, 2014.

"Overall Findings." http://spirituality.ucla.edu/findings/.

"Parliament Bill (Hansard, 11 November 1947)." http://hansard.millbanksystems.com/commons/1947/nov/11/parliament-bill.

Pew Research Center. "'Nones' on the Rise." http://www.pewforum.org/2012/10/09/nones-on-the-rise/.

Pilgrim, Walter E. *Uneasy Neighbors: Church and State in the New Testament.* Minneapolis: Fortress, 1999.

Richardson, Cyril C., trans. and ed. "Epistle to Diognetus." In *Early Christian Fathers,* 216–18. Philadelphia: Westminster, 1953.

Robertson, Pat. "Concerned Citizens Can Return America to Its Roots." http://www.patrobertson.com/speeches/ConcernedCitizens.asp.

Rorty, Richard. *Achieving Our Country: Leftist Thought in Twentieth-Century America.* Cambridge: Harvard University Press, 1999.

————. *Philosophy and Social Hope.* New York: Penguin, 2000.

————. "Religion in the Public Square: A Reconsideration." *Journal of Religious Ethics* 31 (2003) 141–49. doi: 10.1111/1467-9795.00127.

Ruse, Cathy. "What a Trump Court Would Mean for Abortion." *The Daily Signal,* November 29, 2016. http://dailysignal.com/2016/11/29/what-a-trump-court-would-mean-for-abortion/.

Sauvage, Pierre. *Weapons of the Spirit.* Documentary, 1989.

Schuessler, Jennifer. "Hard Truth for Author: Publisher Pulls 'The Jefferson Lies.'" *New York Times*, August 14, 2012. http://artsbeat.blogs.nytimes.com/2012/08/14/hard-truth-for-author-publisher-pulls-the-jefferson-lies/?_r=1.

Segarra, Marielle. "In Pennsylvania, It's Legal to Deny Someone Housing for Being Gay, Lesbian, Bisexual or Transgender." *KeystoneCrossroads.org*, December 18, 2015. http://www.newsworks.org/index.php/local/keystone-crossroads/89250-in-most-of-pennsylvania-its-legal-to-deny-someone-housing-for-being-gay-lesbian-bisexual-or-transgender.

Sider, Ronald J., and Diane Knippers. *Toward an Evangelical Public Policy: Political Strategies for the Health of the Nation*. Grand Rapids: Baker, 2005.

Smith, Gregory A., and Jessica Martínez. "How the Faithful Voted: A Preliminary 2016 Analysis." http://www.pewresearch.org/fact-tank/2016/11/09/how-the-faithful-voted-a-preliminary-2016-analysis/.

Somashekhar, Sandhya. "Study: Abortion Rate at Lowest Point since 1973." *Washington Post*, February 2, 2014. https://www.washingtonpost.com/national/health-science/study-abortion-rate-at-lowest-point-since-1973/2014/02/02/8dea007c-8a9b-11e3-833c-33098f9e5267_story.html.

Springs, Jason, et al. "Pragmatism and Democracy: Assessing Jeffrey Stout's Democracy and Tradition." *Journal of the American Academy of Religion* 78 (2010) 413–48. doi: 10.1093/jaarel/lfq011.

Stark, Rodney. *The Triumph of Christianity: How the Jesus Movement Became the World's Largest Religion*. New York: HarperOne, 2011. Kindle edition.

Stassen, Glen Harold, and David P. Gushee. *Kingdom Ethics: Following Jesus in Contemporary Context*. Downers Grove, IL: InterVarsity, 2003.

"State Same-Sex Marriage State Laws Map." http://www.governing.com/gov-data/same-sex-marriage-civil-unions-doma-laws-by-state.html.

Stetzer, Ed. "Marriage, Divorce, and the Church: What Do the Stats Say, and Can Marriage Be Happy?" *The Exchange*, February 14, 2014. http://www.christianitytoday.com/edstetzer/2014/february/marriage-divorce-and-body-of-christ-what-do-stats-say-and-c.html.

Stout, Jeffrey. *Blessed Are the Organized: Grassroots Democracy in America*. Princeton: Princeton University Press, 2010.

———. *Democracy and Tradition*. Princeton: Princeton University Press, 2004.

Sunshine, Glenn S. *Reforming French Protestantism: The Development of Huguenot Ecclesiastical Institutions, 1557–1572*. Sixteenth Century Essays & Studies. Kirksville, MO: Truman State University Press, 2003.

Taylor, Charles. *A Secular Age*. Cambridge: Belknap, 2007.

Thielen, Martin. *The Answer to Bad Religion Is Not No Religion: A Guide to Good Religion for Seekers, Skeptics, and Believers*. Louisville: Westminster John Knox, 2014.

Thomas, Cal, and Ed Dobson. *Blinded by Might: Can the Religious Right Save America?* Grand Rapids: Zondervan, 1999.

Tocqueville, Alexis de. *Democracy in America*. Edited and translated by Harvey Claflin Mansfield and Delba Winthrop. Chicago: University of Chicago Press, 2000.

u2bheavenbound. "Saddleback Church Rick Warren interviews Barack Obama 2008." https://www.youtube.com/watch?v=N1VwHT9VfQk.

Vine, W. E, et al. *Vine's Complete Expository Dictionary of Old and New Testament Words*. Nashville: Nelson, 1985.

BIBLIOGRAPHY

Waltke, Bruce K., and Cathi J. Fredricks. *Genesis: A Commentary.* Grand Rapids: Zondervan, 2001.

Walton, John H. *The Lost World of Genesis One: Ancient Cosmology and the Origins Debate.* Downers Grove, IL: IVP Academic, 2009.

Walzer, Michael. *Exodus and Revolution.* New York: Basic, 1985.

———. *In God's Shadow: Politics in the Hebrew Bible.* New Haven: Yale University Press, 2012.

———. *Interpretation and Social Criticism.* Cambridge: Harvard University Press, 1993.

———. *The Paradox of Liberation: Secular Revolutions and Religious Counterrevolutions.* New Haven: Yale University Press, 2015.

———. *The Revolution of the Saints: A Study in the Origins of Radical Politics.* Cambridge: Harvard University Press, 1965.

———. *Spheres of Justice: A Defense of Pluralism and Equality.* New York: Basic, 1983.

———. *Thick and Thin: Moral Argument at Home and Abroad.* Notre Dame: University of Notre Dame Press, 1994.

Weatherford, Ronald Jeffrey, and Carole Boston Weatherford. *Somebody's Knocking at Your Door: AIDS and the African-American Church.* Binghamton, NY: Haworth Pastoral, 1999.

West, Cornel. *The Cornel West Reader.* New York: Basic Civitas, 1999.

"What Was the Three-Fifths Compromise?" http://constitution.laws.com/three-fifths-compromise.

Wigram, George V., and Ralph D. Winter. *The Word Study Concordance: A Modern, Improved, and Enlarged Version of Both the Englishman's Greek Concordance and the New Englishman's Greek Concordance.* Wheaton, IL: Tyndale, 1978.

Willard, Dallas. *The Divine Conspiracy: Rediscovering Our Hidden Life in God.* San Francisco: HarperSanFrancisco, 1998.

"William Wilberforce (1759–1833): The Politician." http://abolition.e2bn.org/people_24.html.

Williams, Reggie L. *Bonhoeffer's Black Jesus: Harlem Renaissance Theology and an Ethic of Resistance.* Waco: Baylor University Press, 2014.

Willimon, William H. *What's Right with the Church.* San Francisco: Harper & Row, 1985.

Winslow, Anne Goodwin. *The Dwelling Place.* New York: Knopf, 1943.

Wright, N. T. *Jesus and the Victory of God.* Minneapolis: Fortress, 1996.

Yoder, John Howard. *The Christian Witness to the State.* Newton, KS: Faith and Life, 1964.

———. *For the Nations: Essays Evangelical and Public.* Grand Rapids: Eerdmans, 1997.

———. *The Politics of Jesus: Vicit Agnus Noster.* Grand Rapids: Eerdmans, 1972.

———. *The Priestly Kingdom: Social Ethics as Gospel.* Notre Dame: University of Notre Dame Press, 1984.

Yoder, John Howard, et al. *The War of the Lamb: The Ethics of Nonviolence and Peacemaking.* Grand Rapids: Brazos, 2009.